The

SUBTLE
POWER

—— *of* ——

SPIRITUAL
ABUSE

Books by Jeff VanVonderen

Families Where Grace Is in Place

*Good News for the Chemically Dependent and Those
    Who Love Them*

The Suble Power of Spiritual Abuse (with David Johnson)

Tired of Trying to Measure Up

The
SUBTLE
POWER
of
SPIRITUAL
ABUSE

DAVID JOHNSON
JEFF VANVONDEREN

BETHANY HOUSE PUBLISHERS

Minneapolis, Minnesota

Published by Bethany House Publishers
11400 Hampshire Avenue South
Bloomington, Minnesota 55438

Bethany House Publishers is a division of
Baker Publishing Group, Grand Rapids, Michigan.

Printed in the United States of America

ISBN-13:   978-0-7642-0137-0
ISBN-10:   0-7642-0137-9

Library of Congress Cataloging-in-Publication Data

Johnson, David (David W.), 1952-
    The subtle power of spiritual abuse : recognizing & escaping spiritual manipulation and false spiritual authority within the church / David Johnson & Jeff VanVonderen
        p. cm.
Summary: "Written for both those who feel abused and those who may be causing it, The Subtle Power of Spiritual Abuse shows how people get hooked into abusive systems, the impact of controlling leadership on a congregation, and how the abused believer can find rest and recovery"—Provided by publisher.
    Includes bibliographical references.
ISBN 0-7642-0137-9 (pbk.)
    1. Christianity—Psychology. 2. Christian leadership. 3. Authority—Religious aspects—Christianity. 4. Christian life. I. VanVonderen, Jeffrey. II. Title.
    BR110.J553   2005
    253—dc22

                                                                    2005019948

Dedicated
to the weary and heavy laden,
deeply loved by God,
but because of spiritual abuse,
find that the Good News
has somehow become
the bad news.

Special Thanks from Jeff VanVonderen:

To my mother, Beverly VanVonderen Nyberg. In spite of being surrounded by a shaming religious environment and confused and concerned about my personal struggles, she remained the most unconditionally loving and accepting person in my life.

Special Thanks from David Johnson:

To my father, William Johnson, who through his life and teaching taught me grace and pointed me to Jesus as my only hope. He serves in my life as an example of what it means to open the kingdom of God to people. I am grateful.

To my wife, Bonnie, for knowing and loving me, and for her patience and support on this project.

To my children, Aundrea, Erica, Caleb, and Kristopher for constantly bringing me "home."

DAVID JOHNSON has been the senior pastor at Church of the Open Door in Maple Grove, Minnesota, since 1980. During this time, the church as grown from a congregation of 160 to 3,000 people. A much sought after speaker, he is a graduate of Bethel College and received his theological training at Bethel Seminary and Trinity Evangelical Divinity School. His *Growing in Grace* radio broadcast is syndicated internationally. David and his family live in Minnesota.

JEFF VANVONDEREN is an internationally known speaker on addictions and church and family wellness. He has worked as a counselor in both residential and out-patient treatment settings, as well as in the religious community, taught at the college level, and is the author of several books, including *Good News for the Chemically Dependent and Those Who Love Them*. He is one of the featured interventionists on the A&E documentary series *Intervention* and has appeared on *Oprah*, *The Today Show*, and *Larry King Live*. He makes his home in California.

Contents

Part I

Spiritual Abuse
and Its Victims

Author's Note

As you read through this book, you will notice we have repeatedly emphasized that the subject matter and guidelines given here must be handled with care. Please take this concern seriously. Our stated purpose is to help readers—victims and abusers alike—recognize and escape spiritual manipulation and false spiritual authority within the church.

As some of you read this book, you may find that for the first time you will be able to identify painful feelings long locked within. For others, you may find validation for feelings and perceptions of which you have been aware for a long time, but wondered if you were crazy or way off base. Know this. You can *respond* and not *react*. You can take your time to understand the principles we have detailed and weigh the complete message. If you decide through this material that you have been spiritually abused or are presently in a spiritually abusive situation, it is not necessary nor helpful to strike out at the abusers. Reactions that burst from pain and disappointment often feel good and right at the time. But most often they do not build, they hurt your credibility, and sometimes those reactions incur further abuse. Take your time. Emotional healing will come. There is recovery from spiritual abuse.

And there is appropriate and effective confrontation for spiritual abuse. If you are not able to give it immediately, then with some help, support, and healing, you may be able eventually to respond with a settled assurance that is based upon the truth of God's Word and from a heart that has been renewed by God's love and His Spirit. And your soft heart won't feel the need to apologize for it later.

Introduction

Messages From the Heart

David Johnson:

I was not prepared for the look on the unfamiliar woman's face as she came forward for prayer at the end of a church service. She was teary-eyed, anxious. But most of all, I saw fear. What's more, as she began to speak, it became apparent what she was afraid of—*me!*

Instantly, I wondered what I might have said or done to make this simple step so traumatic for her. As we began to talk, however, I realized that she wasn't afraid of me personally—it was what I represented. I was a pastor, a figure of authority. And not just any authority—a spiritual authority, a "representative of God." She was terrified of that, and coming to me for prayer was one of the hardest, bravest things she'd ever done.

Later, as I pondered the encounter, I realized that she exhibited the characteristics of an abuse victim. But this time the abuse wasn't sexual, physical, or emotional; it was, quite possibly, more serious because in most quarters it is a "taboo" subject. Her abuse was spiritual.

In the context of her Christian home and her evangelical church, this woman had been shamed, manipulated and weighed down by a distortion of the gospel. Though Jesus came with "good news" to set us all free, she had been pressed by other Christians to work harder at being "a good Christian." When she had failed in her honest attempts, she was judged as undisciplined and unwilling—perhaps even unsaved. She tried harder and harder to do all that was prescribed: more Bible reading, more prayer, more financial sacrifice. Finally, exhausted, she had come seeking help. By then she was so sure I, too, was going to judge her that she nearly *could not* ask for help from one more "spiritual authority." The good news had become bad news; the message of life had been distorted until it nearly crushed out her inner life.

The result, for her, was that the concept of grace was lost completely, and church in general was no longer a safe place. As a pastor, I stood in the place of the one before me who had wounded her soul.

In over ten years as pastor at Church of the Open Door, I have consistently endeavored to preach the grace of God as our only hope for spiritual life and power; that God moves toward the broken, comforts the mourning, and satisfies the hungry. We consistently confront the pious pretending of pharisaical legalism. What we have noticed is that wounded people get healed, and religious people get angry.

But it was this one woman who opened my eyes to the impact that unhealthy spirituality can have on men, women and children. Whereas Christ has called us to freedom and rest (Hebrews 4), too many in the body of Christ are not encouraging wounded, struggling people to begin their healing by resting in the grace of God, but rather to work harder for the benefits of salvation. And if these "formulas" are questioned, those in spiritual authority often feel threatened. Protecting a doctrine, or their own position, they turn on the very ones who have come seeking help.

What I see in this, I cannot ignore. I see the symptoms of a disease for which I finally found a name: spiritual abuse.

I don't believe it was coincidence that during the time this woman came to me I was preaching on Matthew 23: This is the passage in which Jesus reveals the marks and the impact of false spiritual leaders, and He declares His mission to protect their victims. As an expository preacher of God's Word, I am constantly looking for flesh-and-blood ways to illustrate the truths found in Scripture. From my encounter, God gave me a visual aid to help me see the kind of person Jesus was fighting for. In this sense, the Word became flesh, and the concept of spiritual abuse came alive to me.

Though some will balk at the very term "spiritual abuse," I believe this illness is more widespread than we think. That's why I have chosen to work on this book. My deepest desire is that this will be a source of help and healing to both victims and perpetrators of spiritual abuse.

Jeff VanVonderen:

Frank had been referred to me by a therapist at a Christian clinic. It seemed he was stuck in his relationship with God, and the therapist thought I could help "unstick" him. I was informed that Frank was extremely reluctant to come and see a minister, but that he would come in for one session, or two at the most.

When Frank came for our appointment, I greeted him and noted that he shook my hand warily.

As we walked toward my office and approached the door, it was almost as if Frank smashed into an invisible barrier. He stopped dead in his tracks, unable to follow me into the office, as if he was not physically capable of entering that particular air space.

It took Frank more than fifteen minutes to actually walk inside my office. Beginning with our first session, and throughout subsequent sessions over the next two years, Frank related a story of incredible spiritual mistreatment.

He had experienced various forms of abuse growing up, ranging from neglect to overt physical and sexual abuse. If this wasn't enough to overcome, over a period of fifteen years he was shamed, manipulated and sexually abused by several of the pastors and Christian counselors from whom he sought help.

As a counselor, I bring to this book my viewpoint on another aspect of the problem of spiritual abuse. Dave Johnson, my colleague at Church of the Open Door, writes about problems of wrong thinking in the areas of *spiritual authority* and *teaching.* I write mainly as a counselor who deals with numerous cases when the wrongful *treatment* of Christians needing emotional and spiritual help has caused further wounding.

We have been ministering together at Church of the Open Door in Minneapolis for over a decade. During that time we have seen some incredibly wounded people. It wasn't until recently, however, that we identified the cause of many of the wounds. Before, we didn't have the words. Today we see that the bulk of our time and energy has been spent helping to heal wounds caused by spiritual abuse. Both Dave and I share an urgency to talk about spiritual abuse *out loud and on purpose* in the Church, for the very reason that many would choose not to.

When one person treats another in a way that damages them physically, we call that physical abuse. Damaging someone through emotional means is called emotional abuse. Brainwashing is a phrase that describes psychological abuse. Spiritual abuse occurs when someone is treated in a way that damages them spiritually. As a deeper result, their relationship with God—or that part of them that is capable of having a relationship with God—becomes wounded or scarred. As this book unfolds we will illustrate various ways in which this happens and offer help to those who have experienced this form of abuse.

We write to help, not to condemn.

Finally, the two of us have some concerns as we write.

First, our intention is to bring grace and liberation to wounded people. But there will also be pain for those who give themselves permission to feel the anger, sadness or grief they have long held within. We're sorry that it will be painful for some to read our book.

Second, we do not intend that insights in this book be used to harm or destroy anyone—even abusers. It's our assumption that many of these people are themselves deceived. Only when a person will not admit sin should further action be taken. *Please handle this material with care.*

On an editorial note, there are many illustrations contained in this book, and we're grateful to those who shared their stories so that others might receive help. Some stories are told as they happened, others have been somewhat altered in detail to protect confidentiality while maintaining the integrity of the story's main point.

Most important, we want to say to those who are victims of spiritual abuse: We have heard the message from your heart. God never intended for you to be abused in His name. He is still for you (Romans 8).

Through this writing, may you come into a renewed, healthy relationship with God!

Spiritual abuse is a real phenomenon that actually happens in the body of Christ. It is a subtle trap in which the ones who perpetrate spiritual abuse on others are just as trapped in their unhealthy beliefs and actions as those whom they, knowingly or unknowingly, abuse.

What is spiritual abuse? How does it occur? Are you a victim?

1

"Help Me..."

Jeri sat in the office of a Christian counselor, explaining that she felt desperate, and felt like she was going crazy. "Either that," she said dryly, "or I'm on the verge of a major breakthrough in my spiritual growth."

"Those are two big opposites," the counselor noted. "How did you come to that conclusion?"

"Well," she began, choking up, "I went to my pastor a few months ago because I was feeling depressed a lot. He pegged the root problem right away, but I can't seem to do anything about it."

"Root problem . . ." the counselor repeated. "What was that?"

Jeri looked down at her shoe tops. "I guess I would have to say the problem is, well, *me*. My pastor says I'm in rebellion against God."

What unfolded was an unfortunate, and all too common, case history: Jeri's church teaches that Scripture is God's Word, the standard by which we must live. But they use it as a measure by which we gain acceptance with God rather than as a guide for living. Therefore, when she asked her pastor for help with her depression, she was given a "prescription" of praise Scriptures to memorize and repeat over and over. This, she was told, would get her mind off herself and onto God. The depression would lift when she got over her sinful self-centeredness.

Jeri had tried what the pastor suggested, but her depression didn't lift, and this raised some questions. She noted that there was a history of depression among the women in her family, and that she was presently experiencing some physical problems. Moreover, she confided to her pastor that she was struggling in her relationship with her husband, because he shrugged off responsibilities with their two teenagers who were beginning to get into trouble.

"How did he respond when you said his suggestion didn't help?"

"That's when he dropped the bomb on me," Jeri said.

The counselor did not fail to notice her choice of metaphor—the devastation Jeri was trying to portray—and asked, "What sort of 'bomb'?"

The pastor had told her, "The fact that you won't accept my counsel without raising all these objections and other possibilities was the major indication to me, Jeri, that your root problem is spiritual, not physical or emotional. When you talked about arguing with your husband, rather than submitting to him and trusting God, that confirmed it." He concluded that the other problems—emotional depression, physical illness, a troubled marriage and teenagers in turmoil—were the *result* of her inability to submit fully to God and His Word.

Jeri had tried to object. "I told him I felt condemned. That I felt I needed some other kind of help."

"What happened?" the counselor prompted.

"That made it worse. My pastor just smiled and said I wasn't willing to accept his counsel—so that proved he was right. That's when he used the 'R' word on me. He said, 'Jeri, you need to repent of your *rebellion* against God. Then all these minor problems will be taken care of.' "

"That's a strong judgment against you," the counselor noted. "What do you think about it?"

Tears welled up, and Jeri dabbed at them with a tissue. Then she sat wringing the tissue in knots as she replied. "I feel like a bug pinned down to a piece of cardboard. I try to praise God—I *do* praise Him. But the problem with my husband and kids goes on and on. And when I'm honest with myself I get mad, because just repeating Scriptures, when our family and our health is falling apart, seems so shallow.

"But then I wake up in the middle of the night, hearing my pastor's words. And I think I must be a terrible Christian—in rebellion, like he said—or my life wouldn't be such a mess. He's right, isn't he? Rebellion *is* a sin we all deal with.

"But the turmoil in me has gone on for four months, and I found myself thinking I should stick my head in our gas oven. And other times I think I must be on the verge of a breakthrough to more 'holiness'—if only I could *praise* enough, or *submit* enough. But I don't think I can stick it out long enough. I just feel exhausted, and like I'm losing my mind.

"I can't carry all this weight any more," she ended, pleadingly. "Help me. . . ."

Jeri's dilemma is similar to countless cases we've encountered, representing a widespread and serious problem among Christians. The problem, as we have come to know it, is that of *spiritual abuse*.

No doubt the term itself will disturb, if not shock, many people, though that is not our intent. Nor is it our intent to be alarmist, though we are sounding a call that a problem exists. Therefore, it's important to define what we mean by *spiritual abuse*, and also to make clear from the start that any one of us can be a victim, and sometimes even a perpetrator without realizing what we are doing.

To begin, let's examine the dynamics at work in Jeri's story.

Anatomy of Spiritual Abuse

We could put our finger on several troublesome factors: Jeri's pastor ignored the physical, emotional and relational dimensions of her problem and took a more narrow, "spiritualized" approach. With little investigation, he assumed he knew Jeri's "root problem," that there *was* a root problem. But there are more subtle factors at work, and the subtlety is exactly what gives them their power to wreak great damage.

First, let's examine the *power* dynamic at work.

Jeri had voluntarily made herself vulnerable by sharing a problem. This assumed, of course, that her pastor was healthier in this same problem area—or at least more knowledgeable—and that he could help. Because she felt weak in this area, help from someone stronger is what she was seeking. Add to that the pastor's position of spiritual authority, and it's easy to see how his words would have double weight in Jeri's thinking.

And then, sadly, help is not what Jeri was offered. This is where a second dynamic comes in: *The focus of the issue was subtly changed.*

Jeri went to talk about her problem of depression. The pastor addressed the problem as being Jeri herself. According to him, she was "rebellious"—so *she* was the problem. He shifted the focus from an emotion to the person, from Jeri's state of feelings to her state of being. Depression was no longer the problem, to be worked through together; Jeri herself was "the problem," labeled a rebel who needed to live up to a standard.

Jeri never noticed that she was not receiving help, which is what she was hoping for. Instead, her spiritual position before God was being questioned and, it would appear, judged.

At the bottom of this sad, painful encounter lies perhaps the subtlest dynamic: Jeri *questioned an authority who considered himself above questioning*, perhaps even above error.

Now in a normal dialogue, for instance, you may misunderstand or disagree with me. If you question my thinking, and in fact your question corrects an error I'm making, then your challenge was healthy for me. It corrected me. But the simple fact that you questioned me does not make you wrong. Unfortunately, a more subtle set of assumptions were at work against Jeri. They went something like this:

This pastor evidently interpreted his position of authority to mean that his thoughts and opinions were supreme. If he said it, her only right response should be to agree—definitely not to object.

Second, it was assumed that Jeri's questions were coming from a wrong spirit, not simply from an honest attempt to have give-and-take dialogue. In other words, the worst was assumed of her, not the best.

More troublesome than that, frankly, was the power play that went on. In a word, Jeri was manipulated. No doubt Jeri's pastor thought he was only being honest and direct with her, trying to "help" her see her problem. Manipulation came into the picture when Jeri asked an honest question and he "pulled rank." The unspoken attitude she met with might best be stated in words like this: *"I'm the authority*, and because I'm the authority my words are not to be questioned. Since you did question, it's proof that *you're wrong."*

What does this attitude reveal? Perhaps insecurity, buried frustration and anger. It also reveals that the pastor was, at least in this encounter, not functioning in a caring position for Jeri's benefit, though she needed him. On the contrary, it appears that *she* was supposed to affirm and bolster *him* by agreeing, regardless of how she felt and whether or not his assessment of her was accurate. Upholding his position of authority was what mattered most.

What Is Spiritual Abuse?

Witnessing the spiritual anguish caused by dynamics like these time after time is what led us to coin the term *spiritual abuse*. Having illustrated it with a case study, now let's define and apply the term:

> *Spiritual abuse is the mistreatment of a person who is in need of help, support or greater spiritual empowerment, with the result of weakening, undermining or decreasing that person's spiritual empowerment.*

That's a broad view. Let's refine that with some functional definitions. Spiritual abuse can occur when a leader uses his or her *spiritual position* to control or dominate another person. It often involves overriding the feelings and opinions of another, without regard to what will result in the other person's state of living, emotions or spiritual well-being. In this application, power is used to bolster the position or needs of a leader, over and above one who comes to them in need. This is what occurred in Jeri's case.

Spiritual abuse can also occur when *spirituality* is used to make others live up to a "spiritual standard." This promotes external "spiritual performance," also without regard to an individual's actual well-being, or is used as a means of "proving" a person's spirituality. What constitutes the kind of "spiritual performance" we are referring to? When does an authority overstep his or her bounds, leveling judgment when support is needed? Listen to the experiences of these Christians, wounded and overweighted by the demands of their leaders and their "spirituality," and you will perhaps get a clearer picture:

"My Bible study leader tells me that I haven't taken on the 'mantle' as spiritual head of my home. I should be praying more, taking *authority* in the Spirit—then spiritual forces wouldn't be able to attack my family. Then my wife wouldn't be having menstrual problems and my oldest son wouldn't be suffering from asthma. I guess their sickness is my fault."

"Quite a number of us wanted more information about how church finances were being spent. We wanted to know if more money could go into direct ministries, benevolences, things like that. When I asked some questions at an elders' meeting—boy did the room get icy. Later I was told to stop trying to create a faction in the church."

"We'd sold our home and moved across country so I could work for this major ministry. After a year they got on this weight thing. Because I'm overweight, I was told I had to lose weight, because being overweight is 'a poor witness.' My financial raises and even my employment were at stake."

"The congregation let me know they were disappointed in me because I asked for a two-month sabbatical, even though I've been pastoring here for twelve years—basically on-call night and day, and I've never even taken two weeks of vacation at the same time. I feel so discouraged."

"Our church has gotten into this heavy emphasis on home schooling and having big families. Also on women wearing head coverings to show they're in submission—and no makeup. Eventually it came out. Our best friends told us we aren't spiritual because our kid is in public schools, and I'm 'of the world' because I wear eyeshadow and lipstick."

"The controversy began—can you believe it?—when I raised a question in the adult Sunday school class. We were batting around a doctrinal issue, predestination, which I always thought of as a 'gray area.' I disagreed with the teacher, in a friendly spirit. But two days later, I was told by the church's ministry coordinator that I'd been 'argumentative' with the teacher in front of everyone—that they would appreciate it if I would drop out of the class until further notice."

"My husband is convinced I should be praying one hour a day, using this 'formula prayer' he's into. I told him I tried that, and it didn't seem right to me. All he said was, 'That's your whole problem. You can't accept anything on faith.' I feel so . . . substandard."

Each of these incidents had similar dynamics at work. The person in need—whether it was the need for information, dialogue, support, acceptance or counsel—was sent the message that they were less than spiritual, or that their spirituality was defective. In several instances, shame was used in an attempt to get someone to support a belief, or it was used to fend off legitimate questions.

Hopefully you noticed, as in the case of the weary pastor, that spiritual abuse can be heaped upon leaders as well as followers. By no means are we attacking *leaders* or *spiritual leadership*. We're exposing a phenomenon that is wounding many.

Whatever the case, the results of spiritual abuse are usually the same: The individual is left bearing a weight of guilt, judgment or condemnation, and confusion about their worth and standing as a Christian.

It's at this point, we say, that spirituality has become abusive.

Is "Abuse" Too Harsh a Word?

Looking at the phenomenon we're writing about from a slightly different perspective may help you to understand why we go so far as to use the term *spiritual abuse*. We are well aware that the term may be controversial, and yet we are also convinced, in light of other ground-breaking counseling in other fields, that the use of the word *abuse* is warranted.

Many are familiar with the recent breakthroughs in "family systems" counseling. Since the church is a "spiritual family made of many families," since it's the family of God, we believe there is something very valuable to learn by looking at the basics of a healthy family system, and what happens when that system becomes unhealthy.

In a healthy, functional family system, the parents occupy a place of authority in order to provide need-meeting relationships, experiences, and messages to the children. Here, parents affirm the personhood of their children, while at the same time becoming ever-wiser in their ability to give appropriate consequences for wrong behavior and teach and encourage in right behavior.

It's true that even a good parent makes mistakes. That doesn't mean he is abusive. Sure he's there, in part, to meet the needs of his children, but he's also a human being who is learning and growing, too.

On the other hand, when a parent uses his or her position to force the children to perform, or uses a too-harsh standard to judge by, or uses the position of power to gratify his or her own needs—for importance, power, emotional or even sexual gratification—then the parent has crossed the line into abuse. The family, which is supposed to be the child's one sure "safe place," becomes an *unsafe* place. The relationships that are supposed to help and support instead use, abuse and tear down. When a child trusts, and then is emotionally, verbally, physically or sexually used for an adult's gratification, that is abuse.

Likewise, those in spiritual positions of authority can violate our trust. It's possible to become so determined to defend a spiritual place of authority, a doctrine or a way of doing things that you wound and abuse anyone who questions, or disagrees, or doesn't "behave" spiritually the way you want them to. When your words and actions tear down another, or attack or weaken a person's standing as a Christian—to gratify you, your position or your beliefs while at the same time weakening or harming another—that is spiritual abuse.

There are spiritual systems in which what people think, how they feel and what they need or want does not matter. People's needs go unmet. In these systems, the members are there to meet the needs of the leaders: needs for power, importance, intimacy, value—really, *self*-related needs. These leaders attempt to find fulfillment through the religious performance of the very people whom they are there to serve and build. This is an inversion in the body of Christ. It is spiritual abuse.

This Is Not a "Witch Hunt"

We've taken some pains to define what spiritual abuse is. It's a real phenomenon, not confined to cults but actually happening (sad to say) in the body of Christ. It's equally important to us that readers understand what spiritual abuse is *not*. It's also important for you to understand this: *Any one of us can unwittingly forget about the empowering grace by which we're to live the Christian life, and to act or speak in a way that spiritually abuses others.* Though readers may identify real situations of abuse in groups or churches in which they're involved, we are not suggesting that anyone start a "witch hunt" to seek and destroy abusers.

Here are some important distinctions to keep in mind:

- It is *not* abusive when a spiritual leader, who has the responsibility to make final decisions, uses his/her best judgment and chooses to go against your opinion. It is abusive, however, if someone's opposing view is used to devalue a person's spirituality.
- It is not abusive when a Christian (whether or not they are a leader) confronts another Christian because of sin, wrongdoing or even honest mistakes that must be corrected. The objective, of course, is not to shame or discredit, but to heal, save and restore.
- Likewise, it is not abusive when a person in ministry or leadership is asked to step down from their position because of emotional, physical, mental or spiritual problems. The goal, however, must be on helping the individual to receive help, so as to eventually return to their office or position if that is the best action.
- It is not spiritually abusive or inappropriate to disagree, whether on doctrines or other issues, even in public. Keep in mind, though, that it is always crucial to maintain respect and never to belittle or attack.
- It is not abusive to hold to certain standards of group conduct (like style of dress). It becomes abusive when others are spiritually degraded or shamed because they do not maintain the same convictions.

What we're saying, in this regard, is that spiritual abuse is a trap. The ones who perpetrate spiritual abuse on others are just as trapped in their unhealthy beliefs and actions as those who they knowingly or unknowingly abuse. And it's important to issue some other warnings:

- A strong leader is not automatically abusive because he or she is strong and decisive.

• A person can be both a victim *and* a perpetrator at the same time. For example, you may feel put down or pressured to "perform" by a Christian leader, and at the same time be judging your teenager for being "in rebellion" when he's only asking you to review some decision that really is unfair, or is naturally trying to check out the belief system you've handed him since he was a baby, trying to make it real for himself. Or a woman can feel victimized or neglected by her husband, who has a heavy-handed approach to spiritual authority in the home, and at the same time be using spirituality to punish her children or to drive them to perform like little angels.

One basic purpose of this book is to help you examine your own practice of Christianity first. Are you practicing grace, allowing the Spirit of Christ to live through you in such a way that you help lift oppressive weights off of others and spiritually empower them to live? Or are you trying to force people to live under laws, rules or formulas for spirituality that cause them to feel weighed down, unable to measure up to your standards?[1]

And there is another important purpose in our writing: It is to help both leaders and followers to recognize spiritual systems that have become abusive. From our widespread contacts with both victims and perpetrators, we know how deeply this problem has scarred the face of Christianity. For those who will discover they've built a system that's spiritually abusive—enslaving people to a system, a leader, a standard of performance—we have some advice and guidance that can help you change and return to grace. And for those who discover they've been stuck in an abusive, enslaving system, we offer advice and guidance on how to make changes that will bring you back to the freedom that's in Christ.

The apostle Paul wrote:

It is for freedom that Christ has set us free. Stand firm, then, and do not let yourselves be burdened again by a yoke of slavery. (Galatians 5:1, NIV)

And also:

You were bought at a price; do not become slaves of men. (1 Corinthians 7:23, NIV)

At the root of it all, we find that too many today have forgotten the

---

[1]Jeff VanVonderen, *Tired of Trying to Measure Up* (Minneapolis: Bethany House Publishers, 1990).

incredible price that was paid, in blood, for our freedom in Christ. For we have been called to a spiritual life built upon the free gift of God's grace (Ephesians 2:8-9). The works we are to do are only those that our God and Father prepared for us (v. 10). It is to God alone whom we will answer for what we have done in His name and what we've failed to do (Matthew 25).

With an Eye Toward Freedom

How does spiritual abuse happen? How can a system that is intended to set people free become a means of bondage and oppression? Is there a parallel in Scripture to help us further understand the dynamics at work here?

Are there signs that identify spiritual abuse—something beneath the anger, distrust, fear, doubt, poor relationships—that can help a counselor recognize when spiritual abuse is the deeper-lying problem?

In the next chapters, we'll explore these foundational questions. Beyond that, we'll look at how to reverse a spiritually abusive system, how to make that system a "safe place" for hurting and growing Christians.

The Christian life *begins* with freedom from dead works, from religious systems and from all human attempts to "please God." It's time for many of us to shake off the religious systems and expectations we've created, and *return to that joyful freedom in Christ.*

Ultimately, that's our hope and our goal.

Both Old and New Testaments warn of false prophets and spiritual systems that add the performance of religious behaviors to the performance of Jesus on the cross as a means to find God's approval. All of us, as Christians, are told to be on our spiritual guard.

Are the spiritual relationships you have bringing the rest Jesus promised, or do you find just more toil and weariness?

2

Spiritual Abuse Is Not New

Spiritual abuse, in fact, is not new. But we believe that the community of faith has, quite possibly, lived so close to the phenomenon that we have felt its symptoms without knowing what exactly was wrong. We struggled at first with the term before we realized, by examining Scripture closely, that Jesus himself collided with the problem head on.

Some years ago, a Christian counselor heard that we had begun using the phrase "spiritual abuse" to describe a certain category of counseling issues. She had phoned to describe one of the most incredibly sad case histories we had ever heard. "Now do you think that my client was—I feel odd even saying this—but do you think *she* was spiritually abused? Do you really think there is such a thing?"

Before we had defined spiritual abuse, we could only identify symptoms; we didn't know exactly what to term it. And even after we began using the phrase "spiritual abuse," we wondered the same thing our counselor friend voiced: *Is there such a thing as spiritual abuse? Are we making a big deal out of nothing?*

Too many experiences since have taught us that spiritual abuse really does exist, that it is far-reaching and that it can be as wounding as other forms of abuse. If you're a counselor, you may balk at that, and we don't mean to minimize sexual, physical or emotional abuse, which certainly leave people with serious wounds. Spiritual abuse, however, puts people at odds with their best Friend. It causes some people to question, doubt, and even run the other direction from their Source. They see their strongest Advocate as their biggest accuser, their Ally as their enemy. For some people, spiritual abuse can have eternal consequences.

But on what authority do we base our claim that spiritual abuse really does exist? As we reexamined the Bible we suddenly saw a "picture" of two opposing spiritual systems: one that is under the reign of God, intending to bring life and freedom to people; one a false spiritual system that is under the rule of men, attempting to drive people so that they perform in religious or "pseudo-spiritual" ways, oblivious to the fact that this drains life and steals power.

A Scriptural Portrait

Spiritual abuse, as a religious dynamic, is not new. There are many instances recorded in the Bible wherein people were abused by those in places of religious authority. Let's look at a few.

In the Old Testament

In Jeremiah 5, the prophet relays a list of God's charges against the house of Israel. Beginning in verse 26 he says, "for wicked men are found among My people . . . they set a trap, they catch men." Here is God's lament over the situation: "An appalling and horrible thing has happened in the land. The prophets prophesy falsely, and the priests rule on their own authority" (vv. 30–31).

Notice that abuse is happening *from a place of religious authority*. Spiritual abuse can only come from a place of power or *perceived* power. In other words, it is possible to be abused by someone who doesn't have any true spiritual authority (the marks of which we will discuss later). The abuser only has to be perceived as someone who has power and authority in order to be in a place of leverage in which their words and actions can wound.

In Jeremiah 6, we begin to see the first of several forms spiritual abuse can take—spiritual neglect. We read:

> For from the least of them even to the greatest of them, every one is greedy for gain, and from the prophet even to the priest everyone deals falsely. And they have healed the brokenness of my people superficially, saying, "Peace, peace," but there is no peace (vv. 13–14).

How sad! The religious leaders are so self-consumed that they don't have time or energy to minister to people's real needs. The people of God are left to make do with the religious leftovers. Today, we might parallel Jeremiah's dilemma by examining our own spiritual setting in which the people of God are so often counseled to ignore their real needs and are offered placebos in the form of easy answers, "try hard" sermons, and the latest "get rich" formulas. As in all unhealthy relationship systems, in a spiritually abusive system the most important thing is how things look. So the ugly and messy relational process of meeting people's real needs gets sacrificed for a better-looking but false peace. Many times, "You just need to tell your problem to the Lord," actually means, "Just don't tell it to me," or "Quit saying it out loud."

In the New Testament

The Gospels present numerous pictures of ways people are hurt by abusive spiritual systems in another way: by legalistic attack. It takes only a superficial reading of the New Testament to see that Jesus was not at odds with "sinners"—the prostitutes, lepers and the demonized—but with the religious system of that day.

In Matthew 23, referring to the religious leaders, Jesus says, "They tie up heavy loads, and lay them on men's shoulders; but they themselves are unwilling to move them with so much as a finger" (v. 4).

Scores of people have come for counseling after being worn down in religious systems where the loads of life were not made easier to carry, but instead they were roped by countless religious performance expectations. Like the poor donkeys in Jesus' day, which were so loaded with packages they could hardly be seen beneath their burden, the needy Christian is easily lost in the religious baggage of the abusive system.

Matthew 9:36 describes the multitudes Jesus was speaking to as "distressed" and "downcast." Both words are employed in a Greek sense that means they were being subjected to a process in which some external force was distressing them and causing them to be downcast. That force was the weight of religious expectations under which they labored in order to stay on God's good side, in accordance with the teachings of the legalists of their day. The result of laboring under such a legalistic system was that the people became tired and downcast. In other words, trying hard only made things worse.

Something in the religious system had to be changed to bring the multitudes into the promised rest of God. In fact, God himself brought the change in the form of a Savior, His own Son, Jesus.

It is possible that Matthew 11 contains one of the best descriptions of Jesus' earthly "job description." If you want to see His stance toward tired, wounded, struggling people, here it is:

Come to Me, all who are weary and heavy-laden, and I will give you rest. Take My yoke upon you, and learn from Me, for I am gentle and humble in heart; and you shall find rest for your souls. For My yoke is easy, and My load is light." (vv. 28–30)

If the spiritual relationships you have in Jesus' name don't give you rest, but rather make you more tired as time goes on, then they aren't representing Jesus' purpose accurately. He came to lift from the backs of tired people the burden of trying hard to earn God's approval.

Two particular parts of Jesus' invitation also provide us with significant insights into the terrible nature of spiritual abuse. The words "heavy laden" refer to that process in which an external force has placed a burden or weight on the people. The word "weary" refers to those in the act of working themselves to the point of exhaustion. It is important to see that, once again, despite their ceaseless efforts, the weariness only grows. Trying hard only makes things worse. The truth is that this type of false spirituality offers a god who does not lift burdens, and who places upon people burdens that are worse. This describes the process of spiritual abuse.

Who Are the Perpetrators Today?

The stories of hundreds of Christians confirm that spiritual abuse is as alive today as it ever was. The means by which it happens now is the same as always: First, there is the neglect of real needs in favor of the "needs" of authority; then legalism replaces rest in God with demands for spiritual performance. Abuse is perpetrated by people in positions of power.

Let's be clear again: Not all strong Christian leaders are abusive, nor are all spiritual systems abusive. It's also possible that healthy leaders and spiritual systems can sometimes, unintentionally, treat people in hurtful ways. There is no such thing as a perfect family or church where people don't ever get hurt. But the difference between an abusive and a non-abusive system is that while hurtful behaviors might happen in both, it is not permissible to talk about problems, hurts and abuses in the abusive system. Hence, there is no healing and restoration after the wound has occurred, and the victim is made to feel at fault for questioning or pointing out the problem.

The Old Testament prophets, Jesus, John the Baptist, Paul and others in the New Testament used certain key words and phrases to confront spiritual abuse and the abusers. An understanding of what was meant in the original context will be very helpful in our present struggle to understand spiritual abuse and how to recover from its ravages.

"Brood of Vipers"

It is clear that Jesus took spiritual abuse very seriously. This can be seen in the words He used to characterize the abusers, which to polite ears sound shocking. He called the religious leaders of His day a "brood of vipers." In Matthew 12 He said, "You brood of vipers, how can you, being evil, speak what is good?" (v. 34). He was even more aggressive in a later confrontation: "You serpents, you brood of vipers, how shall you escape the sentence of hell?" (23:33). Matthew 3:7 shows us that "brood of vipers" are the first words John the Baptist ever said to the religious leaders who were coming to be baptized.

These were incredibly strong words. Acts 28 gives us some indications why so harsh a phrase was used. On Paul's way to stand trial in Rome, the apostle's ship was wrecked on the island of Malta. They were wet and cold, so they built a fire. Then it says:

> But when Paul had gathered a bundle of sticks and laid them on the fire, a viper came out because of the heat, and fastened on his hand. And when the natives saw the creature hanging from his hand, they began saying to one another, "Undoubtedly this man is a murderer!" (vv. 3–4).

Vipers were small snakes that looked very much like sticks, and were thus hard to notice. Sometimes while gathering firewood, people would pick up a viper, thinking it was a stick. Since they were often mistaken as sticks, rather than looking dangerous they actually looked useful. Paul was bitten on the hand by a viper that he thought was a stick. These snakes were very poisonous. A viper bite usually resulted in an extremely painful death. That's why the natives thought Paul must have been a murderer. Only a murderer would have deserved the agonizing death Paul was about to die. Even worse, vipers didn't just bite their victims; they latched on and wouldn't let go. Further, they multiplied quickly and congregated in large numbers. You could find "broods" of them in cooler places in the desert, such as in caves and under trees. A desert traveler who was looking for safety and shelter would search out these cooler locations to camp. Unfortunately, the spot that looked as if it offered coolness and rest sometimes offered instead a slow death to the victim who had overlooked a brood of vipers. The place that was supposed to be the safest often turned out to be the least safe place.

Translated into a contemporary metaphor, the word picture Jesus painted would look like this: When a man or woman is going through a dry time in life, lost and tired and searching out a cool, safe place to rest, they need some good news, some living water. They go to church, the place that is supposed to be the safest—after all, didn't the Lord say if we came to Him, He would give rest? In church, the weary soul encounters people who look safe, who seem genuinely interested in helping. These people have their relationships with God together; they are the most concerned about what God wants. But then they inject their venom of performance-based religion and the seeker finds that their strength, health and very spiritual life is sapped. When the person wants to leave, the "vipers" latch on and won't let go.

"Where then is that sense of blessing you had?" Paul asks a group of tired Christians who had fallen victim to spiritual "vipers" in Galatia (Galatians 4:15). If you have ever experienced a performance-based religious system, you know the answer to that question. Remember when you first became a Christian—that joyful moment when you knew that you were forgiven? God's approval was yours, because you were His. You felt light and free. What a relief! Where did that sense of freedom go? It disappeared when you started believing those people who taught you to measure God's acceptance by external religious standards instead of by the Cross. You lost your sense of blessing, and now the harder you try the more tired you become.

Ravenous Wolves

"Beware of the false prophets, who come to you in sheep's clothing, but inwardly are ravenous wolves," Jesus says in Matthew 7:15.

The phrase "ravenous wolves" is being used in the same passage in which Jesus speaks about the wide and the narrow gates by which people enter in search of inner life. Most Christians hear sermons on this text that define "entering by the wide gate" as following the ways of the "world"—that is, going to worldly movies, reading dirty magazines and frequenting bars. Conversely, "entering by the narrow gate" means going to church, reading the Bible, memorizing Scripture, getting perfect Sunday school attendance pins, visiting people in nursing homes, and giving money. The narrow and wide gates are reduced to lists of things we are supposed to do or not do. However, the context reveals a different meaning. Jesus was talking about false prophets— those who looked like they represented God but spoke falsely. Like the true prophets, those prophets stood in front of a wide gate marked "Find Life Here," but this was the gate of religious performance and self-effort, and there was no life on the other side, just toil and weariness.

True prophets stand in front of a narrow gate—the one that says "Come to Me, all who labor. . . ." You can only fit through this gate if you drop all of your "works" baggage and come through alone. On the other side you find heavenly rest. If you try to go through with your perfect attendance pins and Bible quiz trophies, or any of your own righteousness, you simply won't fit. Jesus is the narrow gate. Religion always teaches that you can get to God by doing something. Your good standing with God depends on what you do. Do the law, perform religion, do it right, look good, try hard. Is that the gate through which we are called to find life? No. Those leading people to it are ravenous wolves in sheep's clothing. They look like sheep, and they appear to be the safest, most righteous, but they lead people down the wrong path. Jesus *plus anything* is not Jesus!

It's worse than this, however. In Matthew 10:6, Jesus sends the disciples to the lost sheep of the house of Israel. Where are the lost sheep? They're in the house! Then in verse 16 He gives a warning, "I send you out as sheep in the midst of wolves." Take note: Where are the wolves? They're in the house! A concerned apostle Paul, in preparing to leave Ephesus, says in Acts 20, "I know that after my departure savage wolves will come in among you, not sparing the flock; and *from among your own selves* men will arise" (v. 29, emphasis added).

The most chilling part of this scenario are the words "in sheep's clothing." I used to imagine this as a false sheep that mingles with the flock and occasionally whips off its costume to eat one of the real sheep. Unfortunately, this picture greatly minimizes the damage done by the wolves.

It is true that the destruction is done from within the flock, but it is done by false shepherds, not false sheep. True shepherds sheared the sheep in order to weave the wool into garments. But the false shepherds—wolves—devour the flock in order to get their sheep's clothing. This does not mean merely losing a sheep every once in a while. These false shepherds are leading entire flocks of sheep down the path of destruction.

> There is a conspiracy of her prophets [religious leaders] in her midst, like a roaring lion tearing the prey. They have devoured lives; they have taken treasure and precious things; they have made many widows in the midst of her. Her princes within her are like wolves tearing the prey, by shedding blood and destroying lives in order to get dishonest gain. (Ezekiel 22:25, 27)

"Beware of the false prophets," Jesus warned in Matthew 7:15. The wolves are in the house, and some of them are in charge.

Little wonder that it was part of Jesus' mission to expose an abusive system. It's important to remember four things about His confrontations. First, His confrontations landed on those who saw themselves as God's official spokespersons—the most religious, the best performers. They gave money, attended church and had more Scripture memorized than anyone. They set the standard for everyone else. Second, Jesus broke the religious rules by confronting those in authority out loud. Third, He was treated as the problem because He said there was a problem. And fourth, crowds of broken people rushed to Him because His message offered hope and rest.

Paul's Battle

In his writings to the church, Paul also used a variety of terms to confront those who were spiritually abusing the people of God, including: the circumcision, Judaizers, the false circumcision, the dogs, the evil workers and the false brethren.

Perhaps the most illuminating example showing us the dynamic of spiritual abuse is Paul's example in the book of Galatians. During his first missionary journey, Paul had preached the Good News of life and forgiveness in Christ in an area called Galatia. People were gloriously saved by placing their faith in Jesus. He later revisited the area to reinforce the faith of those who believed in Christ. It was then he learned that a group of people had followed behind him and spread a teaching that demanded the people be circumcised as an added proof of their spirituality.

In that day, of course, circumcision was the ultimate act of external religious performance. Abraham had been circumcised, but as an outside expression of the internal reality of his faith. The act itself had little to do with his standing spiritually. In Genesis 15:6, we read that he *believed God* and God "reckoned it to him as righteousness." The teaching that came to Galatia after Paul's departure was contrary to what he had taught, as well as a distortion of the original intent of circumcision. Consequently, he was dismayed and even indignant.

Therefore, a spiritual system to be avoided is one in which the leaders or teachers add the performance of religious behaviors to the performance of Jesus on the cross as the means to find God's approval. The teaching of the Judaizers went something like this: "Faith in Jesus is right, and you must have it. But it's not enough. In order to really find positive standing in God's eyes, you have to be circumcised." In others words, false spiritual systems teach that right standing with God depends on what Jesus did, *plus* those "spiritual" acts that you do.

Legalism

The weight we are describing is called *legalism*. It is a form of religious perfectionism that focuses on the careful performance and avoidance of certain behaviors. It teaches people to gain a sense of spiritual acceptance based on their performance, instead of accepting it as a gift on the basis of Christ.

Why were the leaders of Jesus' and Paul's day spreading legalistic teaching? Was it simply a matter of being right? It's more serious than that. Look at Galatians 6:12–13:

> Those who desire to make a good showing in the flesh try to compel you to be circumcised, simply that they may not be persecuted for the cross of Christ. For those who are circumcised do not even keep the Law themselves, but they desire to have you circumcised, that they may boast in your flesh.

You see, living with Jesus as your only source of life and acceptance is a confrontation to those who seek God's approval on the basis of their own religious behavior.

This, then, explains the pressure you feel to perform religious behaviors in spiritually abusive contexts. If you perform as they say you must: (1) it will make them look good; (2) their self-righteousness will escape the scrutiny of the cross of Christ as the only means to God's favor; (3) it will allow them to examine you instead of themselves; (4) they will be able to "boast in" or gain a sense of validation from your religious performance.

Can you see the abusive dynamic described in chapter one? Here we have religious people trying to meet their own spiritual needs through someone else's religious performance. And it's all cloaked in the language of being holy and helping others to live holy lives.

Paul catalogs the damage at Galatia throughout the book of Galatians. In 1:7 he says they were "disturbed," the meaning of which ranges from "thrown into mental confusion" to "urged to commit treason." In 2:4 Paul calls this false teaching an attempt to "bring us into bondage." In 3:1 he says they were "bewitched," which means they acted as if they had a spell put on them. In 4:29 he calls what has happened to the Galatians "persecution." In 5:7 he says they were "hindered from obeying the truth." And in 4:15 he asks the sad and telling question, to both them and us, "Where then is that sense of blessing you had?"

People who are spiritually abused feel so tired and so belittled, because they cannot live up to other's spiritual expectations, that they have lost their sense of blessing.

A Seething Confrontation

While the words Paul uses to describe the abuse are vivid, his confrontation is seething. Paul says, "I am amazed that you are so quickly deserting Him who called you by the grace of Christ, for a different gospel; which is really not another; only there are some who are disturbing you, and want to distort the gospel of Christ" (Galatians 1:6–7).

When someone deserts from the army, they are Absent Without Official Leave. The Greek word for "desert" does not mean "absent." It means to "defect." When someone defects, they go over to the side of the enemy. In other words, those who are "disturbing" you are urging you to commit treason. Note, too, defection is not from denomination or doctrine, but from "Him" who called you by grace.

Paul told the Galatians that if any person, even an angel from heaven, or even Paul himself, were to preach a gospel contrary to (*other* than, or *more* than) the one they had first heard and received, "let him be accursed," or consigned to destruction.

In short, Paul took it very seriously when someone replaced the spiritual life of grace and rest with a life of imposed works.

Leaders Who Serve and Protect the Flock

In 1 Timothy, Paul writes to a young pastor Timothy, leader of the flock at Ephesus. He told Timothy to "instruct certain men not to teach strange doctrines." Was Timothy battling secular humanism? The New Age movement? No, as verse 6 explains, "For some men, straying from these things, have turned aside to fruitless discussion, wanting to be teachers of the Law, even though they do not understand either what they are saying or the matters about which they make confident assertions." In 1 Timothy 6:5 he warns that these erring teachers "suppose that godliness is a means of gain." They act godly not because they *are* godly, but to gain something. "But," Paul says, "godliness actually is a means of great gain, when accompanied by contentment"

(v. 6). Have you ever met a contented legalist, a truly restful religious "performer"? No such person.

In Titus 1:9–10 Paul says:

> An overseer [leader] must hold fast the faithful word [the word that is full of faith] which is in accordance with the teaching, that he may be able both to exhort in sound doctrine and to refute those who contradict. For there are many rebellious men, empty talkers and deceivers, *especially those of the curcumcision, who must be silenced* because they are upsetting whole families. (italics added)

Leaders are given to the church to protect the flock from legalists who push religious performance as the means to right standing or favor with God. Paul tells Titus that the rebellious men must be silenced. Unfortunately, in many churches, not only are the leaders *not* protecting the flock against those who push religious performance, they are the pushers and in bondage to performance themselves. Perhaps that's why people in a lot of churches—the leaders especially—are so tired, shamed and wounded.

Conclusion

It's not wrong to notice legalism, legalistic families and churches, and to protect yourself from being abused. Noticing a problem does not make you the problem. Remember, Paul urged the Ephesians to "be on guard for yourselves and for all the flock" (Acts 20:28).

We believe that all of us, as Christians, need to be on guard—not only against specific leaders and systems that throw their spiritual weight around, but against the subtle use of "formulas" and doctrines that are so often used to press good people of the faith into conformity with a religious system instead of conformity to Christ.

In the following chapter we will look at some of the symptoms present in Christians who are being pressed into conformity in an ungodly system.

It usually comes as a surprise to people who have been spiritually abused when they find that they have a lot in common with other victims. Distorted pictures of God and self, difficulty trusting those in authority, problems understanding and accepting grace are just some of the struggles shared. But since most have had so much pressure to not talk about their experience, they feel alone, even crazy.

Read on and you will find that you are not alone or crazy. You have simply experienced fallout common to the phenomenon of spiritual abuse.

3

Abused Christians

How would you picture a Christian who is growing in godliness? Would they convey *restfulness*, which comes from being comfortable and at peace with God? Would they convey a sense of *fulfillment*, knowing that whatever spiritual work they were doing was in God's will, instead of feeling they had to keep striving for more perfection? Would their advice begin by directing you to Jesus, or would it cause you to focus on yourself and your behaviors? And, ultimately, would this Christian bring with them a sense of life, which Paul describes as the "sweet fragrance of Jesus Christ" (2 Corinthians 2:15, AMP)?

What follows are the ten most common areas of struggle for those who have been spiritually abused. Some victims don't experience all of these symptoms. Others experience symptoms in other areas besides these, but all tend to experience more than a few of the ones listed here. When a person is struggling with one or more of these issues, we consider the possibility that they were spiritually abused. Perhaps these are issues you struggle with, too.

Victims of Spiritual Abuse Struggle in These Areas

You develop a distorted image of God.

Richard grew up in a rigid, authoritarian, religious family and church. The overriding preoccupation of every Christian man, woman and child was to somehow decipher God's will for every area of life, down to whether or not it was in His will to have a certain soft drink. God would be angry if you guessed wrong or failed.

Richard remembers times when, after "laying fleeces" and agonizing in prayer, he would think he'd actually found God's will for him. "It's funny," he said one day. "Whenever I thought I'd figured out God's will, I also immediately thought He then changed it to something different than what I'd guessed, just to keep me from becoming lazy. Knowing what He knew somehow put me on His level, too. God certainly didn't want *that*, so He always kept one step ahead."

It's easy to see how a distorted emphasis on one aspect of spiritual growth became projected onto God himself, so that God became a demanding and fickle authority. Richard and those in his church had to work hard just to keep up spiritually. No wonder Richard soon believed God was like an unfair judge in a horrible road race who kept moving the finish line.

A distorted image of God is one tip-off that someone may have experienced spiritual abuse. Here are some distortions people frequently have:

- As in Richard's case, a God who is never satisfied, who keeps setting higher and higher goals and is eager to let you find out how much you've missed the mark.
- A mean, vindictive God, who is waiting for us to make a mistake. Then He is able to do what He would rather do anyway, which is to point out all our failures, or to punish and humiliate.
- An apathetic God who watches when people are hurt and abused, but does nothing to help because it would mean having to challenge an authority figure or structure.
- A God who is asleep, and doesn't even notice when people are hurt and abused.
- A God who is awake, close, and who sees and cares, but is powerless to help when people are hurt and abused.
- A God who is a kind of fickle baby. His mood can be manipulated by our slightest mistake.
- The "utterly holy" God. He is like a spiritual burglar alarm, ready to go off anytime you think about sin. One man told of a Bible teacher who drilled into him the idea that the Holy Spirit "flees to the farthest corner of the universe whenever you commit the slightest sin, because you've broken His heart."

No doubt many will object to our raising questions about something so simple as Sunday school songs. But if the song conveys the idea that when we are tempted or we sin we have "disappointed" God, when in fact God is the very fountainhead of spiritual strength, restoration and love—the one to whom we should run when we're tempted or we've fallen—then with that in mind, consider the words to this Sunday school song:

Be careful little eyes what you see.
Be careful little eyes what you see.
For the Father up above is looking down in love,
So be careful little eyes what you see.

Now we're not saying that anyone who teaches this song to children is spiritually abusive. But we have to question: Does it reflect a mentality about God that would draw people to Him, or rather cause them to feel shamed by Him because of their weakness? What kind of loving father does a child have to be careful around? What will happen to this child if she or he is *not* careful? What happens if, after trying real hard, this child still hears or sees something he shouldn't? Is this actually a "stay away from God" song? Do we want our children to watch out for God, or to run into His arms for strength to overcome?

- There is also the distorted image that results in the "Santa Claus God." This God can be understood by inserting His name into the famous Christmas carol:

You better watch out, you better not cry.
You better not pout, I'm telling you why.
Santa God is coming again.
He's making a list, and checking it twice.
Gonna find out who's naughty or nice.
Jesus Christ is coming again.

He sees you when you're sleeping.
He knows when you're awake.
He knows when you've been bad or good.
So be good for goodness sake.

Please don't be offended, we mean no disrespect. But how many churches teach that your place in heaven will be determined by how many good works you've done here on earth? How many teach that while your *salvation* is not dependent upon works, your *position* close to or far from Him is dependent upon works? How many teach that Jesus' promise of rewards (Matthew 25:31–46) was more than just entry into heaven or dismissal into hell, but a better place in some eternal hierarchy? Santa is the one whose gifts depend upon our behavior. God is the one who gives good gifts simply because He loves us (Luke 11:13), not because of our performance. This leads to the next indication.

You may be preoccupied with spiritual performance.

At a recent Christian conference, it was evident that what was being taught was not growth in a relationship, but adherence to a "formula." This conference put every possible area of life into neat little Christian packages: If you do such and such (read your Bible, memorize Scripture, pray a certain way or for a set amount of time, etc.), God will always be pleased, and the result will always be a nice, packaged, orderly Christian life. People left the seminar resolving to try hard to do the formulas. Those who were successful—which tended to be the already naturally disciplined, strong-willed people—were fortunate to be allowed to attend an advanced seminar.

What about the unsuccessful? They were destined to return to the basic seminar over, and over, and over again. Some people were seven-time repeaters. The speaker told the audience, "If you follow these principles and they don't work, call me and tell me about it. You need to know, though, that you'll be the first one for whom they didn't." No doubt this statement got a lot of people trying very hard to do the formulas. It probably kept even more people from calling.

Preoccupation with spiritual performance often results in a tendency toward extremes of self-righteousness or shame. Self-righteousness (a sense of spiritual superiority based on your own behavior) and judgmentalism (a sense of spiritual superiority based upon someone else's behavior) indicate a performance-based lifestyle. Another indicator is perfectionism, or a need for situations and relationships to be "just so." This is often accompanied by a high level of anxiety based upon external circumstances and an urge to control what people do and how things turn out.

Shame, the flip side of self-righteousness, is also a result of a performance-based mentality. Shame is a sense of inferiority, a negative self-assessment, an indictment on your very personhood. It results from experiencing relationships where love and acceptance are based upon behaviors, and where the constant message is that you don't measure up.

In spiritual systems where performance is more important than emotional honesty or human need, both extremes will be strongly in evidence.

You have a distorted self-identity of yourself as a Christian.

People who have been spiritually abused tend to have a negative picture of self, or a shame-based identity. This can be seen in several ways:

- Lack of understanding or even awareness of New Testament texts that elaborate on our identity as new creations in Christ.
- Confusion between guilt and shame. *Guilt* is a valuable signal indicating a wrong or bad behavior. *Shame* is an indictment on you as a person. You experience guilt when you do a wrong behavior; guilt is a good spiritual nerve ending causing you to right wrong behavior. You feel shame even when you've done nothing wrong; you feel defective as a human being, and like a third-rate Christian undeserving of God's blessings and acceptance.
- Shame is the prime motivator of behavior; i.e., the dilemma of your negative picture of self can only be solved by good behavior.
- A high need to hang on to a negative picture of self in order to explain negative behaviors. This is true of spiritual systems that teach or insinuate that even though you are saved you're still "worthless" before God, "just a sinner saved by grace," "a worm and not a person."

Consider the subtle message about your identity communicated in the following popular chorus:

I am so glad that Jesus loves me, Jesus loves me,
Jesus loves me.
I am so glad that Jesus loves me.
Jesus loves *even* me.

This song insinuates that Jesus loves a lot of people—but loving *you* was really a stretch. Romans 5:6, however, indicates that everyone was equally in need of His love. Look at Paul's prayer for everyone whom Jesus loves in Ephesians 3:14–19:

For this reason, I bow my knees before the Father, from whom every family in heaven and on earth derives its name, that He would grant you, according to the riches of His glory, to be strengthened with power through His Spirit in the inner man; so that Christ may dwell in your hearts through faith; and that you, being *rooted and grounded in love, may be able to comprehend with all the saints what is the breadth and length and height and depth, and to know the love of Christ which surpasses knowledge*, that you may be filled up to all the fullness of God.

God didn't *even* love you. He *so* loved you.

You may have a problem relating to spiritual authority.

Being spiritually abused can lead to "toxic faith."[1] Toxic faith is a destructive and dangerous relationship with a religious system, not with God, that allows this system to control a person's life in the name of God. One of the many areas into which this would spill is the area of relating to those in authority.

Those who have experienced the misuse of power develop ways to defend themselves from being abused again. They tend to the extremes of compliance or defiance when faced with someone else having authority. The compliant will conform to the wishes of the one in authority, going along with the authority *whether or not they agree, and whether or not the authority is right.* They comply because the authority requires compliance. It promises to prevent them from getting hurt—but it doesn't. The defiant may resist those who have power, even if they agree on the inside. Their resistance is almost a kneejerk reaction to anyone in charge. This, too, is designed to prevent hurt—but it won't.

You may have a hard time with grace.

The idea of being treated gracefully (treated to a fullness of grace) causes you great difficulty. This springs from the shame-based identity, which tells you that you don't deserve to be treated this way. You find ways to push away the grace extended by God and the gifts from other people, so that you end up going without. Or you accept them with such an overwhelming sense of owing that you find ways to "pay back" God and others for what they've done.

For Christians who have been taught an unbalanced idea about the way holiness comes into a believer's life, there will be an automatic rejection of living under grace—really drawing upon grace daily—as nothing more than "cheap grace," sensing that others are lazy, or are taking advantage of God, or are getting off the hook too easily. If you have to work, others should as well.

You may have a problem in the area of personal boundaries, an unclear understanding about "death to self" teachings and "rights."

Have you ever stayed on the telephone longer than you wanted with a salesperson who was trying to sell something you already knew

---

[1]Stephen Arterburn and Jack Felton, *Toxic Faith* (Nashville, Tenn.: Oliver-Nelson Publishers, 1991).

you weren't going to buy? Why didn't you hang up? Was it because you felt vaguely responsible to make sure he or she didn't feel sad or rejected? What gave this total stranger the right to put his or her uninvited voice in your ear? If you had hung up as soon as you knew you weren't interested, would you have felt guilty, selfish or as if you were a bad Christian (that is, would you have felt shame)? All of this indicates a struggle with boundaries. You *should*, after all, let someone monopolize your life because you're learning "death to self," your life is "not your own," you have "no rights." Right?

Boundaries are invisible barriers that tell others where they stop and you start. The door on your house is a boundary. The lock you turn when you leave for the day is a message to everyone else that you get to decide if they enter or not. While you probably don't feel unspiritual for locking the door to your house (or maybe you do), you would probably feel very unspiritual for saying "No thank you" to a fellow Christian who asked if they could give you a "word from the Lord."

People who have misused their spiritual power have disrespected or beaten down your boundaries. They have shamed you out of your "no," clouded your will and intruded into your life with religious agendas. They have violated your spirituality by playing "Holy Spirit." Having an opinion has come to equal lack of submissiveness. Having a right to *not* be abused is selfish.

You may have difficulty with personal responsibility.

If you've been spiritually abused, you may tend to the extreme of being under-responsible in your relationship with God and others. This simply means that you have realized that no amount of performance results in the promised prize of love, acceptance or rest. Therefore you either decide to give up, or you expend the least amount of energy possible in order to just get by. Inwardly, your attitude is, "Let the pastor visit the sick, let the evangelist witness to the lost—I've *had* it!"

On the other hand, you may have learned to be overresponsible, a burden bearer. Everyone's issues are yours to solve. Their heavy feelings are yours to fix. You have an impossible time saying no to people's needs or requests. After all, if you don't do it, who will? You have a greater sense of God needing *you* than of you needing *God*. In fact, not only are you responsible for how everybody else's day goes, you are even responsible for God's day too. It is your job to live just right, so that God can feel pleased at the end of the day.

The most extreme form of overresponsibility happens when you martyr yourself. You believe that having needs or opinions is selfish. Being affected by insults and thoughtless actions is immature, and having any feelings is being oversensitive. Going without is a prime virtue. Feeling numb to life is the end result.

Matthew 9:36 describes the multitudes as "distressed" and "downcast." This was a result of the performance weight placed on them by the religious leaders who did not shepherd them, but devoured them instead. They did this by endless spiritual rules and regulations, and by constantly pointing out the least flaw in others. If you've been through this, you wind up very tired, emotionally, physically and spiritually. This may show up in the form of lack of energy or motivation, impatience with the needs of others, depression, a sense of being trapped, or finding ways to escape.

You may suffer from a lack of living skills.

Through the years I (Jeff speaking) have counseled many people who were unemployed or underemployed and who were struggling with job and career issues. Many of them were graduate and postgraduate-level people. But in that group I noticed a number of graduates of Christian colleges who were wandering around ill-equipped and jobless, years after graduation. Most were simply the end product of the educational process within a spiritually abusive system.

As you will see in the next chapter, abusive systems develop a "bunker mentality." This is characterized by being closed and paranoid toward the outside, and secretive about what goes on inside. The mentality is not only separatist, but highly judgmental. With this mentality, many Christians may think only one or two colleges are "separate enough" from the world for students to be able to safely attend. Or college education is looked down upon altogether. The result is that a student is equipped emotionally, spiritually, and mentally to work only somewhere in the original system or in one like it. Even though many of these graduates are financially on the brink of disaster, they often hesitate to leave because they aren't able to function in another system. When they finally do leave—because their family is lacking or because they're tired of being mistreated—they are forced to take low-paying jobs in the regular work force. In the eyes of their own, they are considered to have "missed God's call." Spiritually abusive systems like this can produce a lot of college-educated common laborers.

Let me quickly clarify. First, there is no disgrace in being a laborer.

A laborer who depends on Jesus will do as much damage to the gates of hell as a minister who depends on Jesus. The disgrace is in promising people the benefits of a college degree, then giving them a second-rate education and charging them as if it were first-rate. Second, there are many people educated in religious settings who have a first-rate education. There is nothing inherently wrong with home-schooling your kids or sending them to private Christian elementary, secondary or post-graduate schools. In fact, the concept of a first-rate education that includes the component of building people in their faith is wonderful.

The danger is in educating people in religious settings as a result of a "bunker mentality." People who think this way act as if contact with the evil things present in "the world" are the reason people have problems. The solution, therefore, is finding ways to keep people isolated from contact with the world. This is naive at best and, more probably, dangerous. For people whose lives and relationships aren't working, it's important that they come to understand their problem isn't the evil that surrounds them on the outside. Their need is to develop maturity, strength and the ability to make wise decisions, to grow in dependence upon God as their source *on the inside.*

You may have a hard time admitting the abuse.

This is common among spiritual abuse victims for several reasons. In an abusive system, you are told that you are "the problem" for noticing that there is a problem. That makes it hard to expose the abuse, even after you've left the system.

Second, admitting the abuse out loud—or even *thinking* that what you experienced was abuse—often feels like you're being disloyal to family, to church, even to God.

Third, those who have experienced spiritual abuse as "normal" have lost track of what normal really is. Therefore, to call it spiritual abuse feels crazy or overreactive.

Natural human denial is another factor. Denial is actually a God-given ability to delay feeling strong emotional, psychological or spiritual pain. We are not talking about conscious forms of denial, like lying, blaming, minimizing, or rationalizing. We are referring to the automatic numbness that occurs when the amount of pain associated with a situation is too much to bear all at one time. People who experience spiritual abuse often can't believe it is happening to them. It is so inconsistent with everything that is supposed to be happening in families and churches that the excruciating pain of it is short-circuited.

A most serious and most intriguing extreme of this is *repression.* We have seen spiritually abused people, as well as people who were abused in other ways, who have started out in counseling with no recollection of the past abuse. What happened to them was beyond anything they had the capacity to consciously process. It became buried deep in their minds and they literally don't and can't remember. Then some event cracks the denial, and memories begin to trickle—then flow. We have also seen spiritually abused people who get extremely agitated or afraid when talk approaches their past family or church experiences, even though they have no concrete memories of abuse. In this case, their response is like an emotional negative programming.

Finally, there is shame. Once a person is no longer in an abusive situation things become much clearer. They can't believe they didn't see it sooner. Very often they experience a great deal of shame—a sense of defectiveness—for having allowed themselves to get into a situation that was so obviously abusive.

You may have a hard time with trust.

Mark Twain once mused, "A cat that sits on a hot stove lid won't ever sit on a hot stove lid again. But it probably won't sit on a cold stove lid either." Those who have been spiritually abused will have a hard time trusting a spiritual system again. This is extremely significant, because the essence of living as a Christian is a trust relationship with God, within God's family.

Conclusion

It seems hard to believe that Christians, who have answered Jesus' invitation to life and freedom, could so quickly return to a treadmill kind of spirituality that produces soul-deadening weariness. Yet the reasons for this are clear and easy to understand. In part, the answer lies in what we call "the pre-abuse set-up," which we will now examine.

The perpetrator of any abuse is ALWAYS responsible for the abuse. Yet there are two questions that need to be asked. Why do some people stay in abusive relationships? And how do they get into them in the first place?

The answers lie in the fact that people learn unhealthy living skills in unhealthy relationships that actually predispose them for future abuse. Let's look at the "set-up."

4

The Pre-Abuse Set-up

A timid mother and her two frightened-looking daughters huddled fearfully on the sofa as we began our counseling appointment.

"Why did you make this appointment?" I asked (Jeff speaking). From the way they shifted in their seats, I felt that somehow I asked too loudly.

The mother told me her marriage was in trouble. She went on to paint several pictures of abuse by her husband. Then she would take it all back, saying, "Now I don't want you to get the wrong idea. He's a good man." The longer she talked the more serious the abuses she portrayed. Horrible physical abuses.

Finally, the younger of the two girls looked at her mom with tears in her eyes, and blurted, *"Why do you stay with him?"*

"I don't know," came Mom's sobbing response. "I just don't know."

The sad thing is, I have counseled numerous clients exhibiting similar fears, intimidation and undermined will who have been brought to such intense distress by an abusive Christian leader or church system. They feel caught. They desperately want to leave, but they cannot. Somehow they feel hooked.

Why do people stay in spiritually abusive relationships? The abuse victims I have counseled give many reasons:

- There is too much at stake to leave—friends, the years invested, people's opinions.
- They are afraid. They are terrified by the perpetrator's threats to harm them, hurt their parents, or take the kids if they leave.
- They have become so dependent on the abusive system that they don't know if they could leave and survive emotionally or financially.

- They feel they are to blame for inciting the abuse, and they are only getting what they deserve.
- Just about the time they decide to leave, things improve for a while, so they keep changing their mind.
- They believe things about themselves, their relationships, or God that are untrue.

There are two emotional currents that run even deeper than these conscious reasons. First, the victim stays because they are literally powerless to leave. Second, they stay because the spiritually abusive system is a trap. The picture that develops is one of a *powerless person* and an *abusive system* that "fit" with each other.

Being powerless to leave is most easily seen in the case of children, the aged, or vulnerable people like the sick or disabled. That is why there are laws requiring helping professionals to report abuse or suspected abuse of people in these categories. In most cases they are simply not strong enough to advocate for themselves, so someone must advocate for them. But is the concept of advocacy necessary for adults, as well?

Yes. The difference for adults, however, is that their lack of power is what we call "learned powerlessness." Somewhere in their lives they have either had their power stolen from them, or they have not learned the skills needed to *not* be victimized. This is as true in the spiritual arena as it is in any other context where people are abused. The behaviors and attitudes that keep people in abusive systems become much easier to recognize once we understand what learned powerlessness is.

Learned Powerlessness

To fully grasp how a person experiences learned powerlessness, the phenomenon must be seen as a two-sided coin. On one side of the coin is the person who has not learned the skills needed to act capable, competent, and strong. This is due to the lack of opportunities and support to do so in their past and present relationship systems. At best, they are *survivors*, but they do not prosper and grow as individuals. Expecting them to flourish in life would be comparable to asking a third-grade Pee Wee baseball player to compete on a high school baseball team. They will fail because they are not capable, although they will probably survive.

Have you ever been to the circus and seen how a huge elephant can be restrained by a piece of rope tied to a tiny wooden stake in the ground? This is possible because the elephant was held captive like that as a baby. The rope and stake came to represent a force it could not overcome. Now, even though it has the strength to easily free itself, it remains a hostage to a tiny stick. This leads us to the second side of "the coin," and that is when a person becomes accustomed to "martyr" behavior. This is the person who has become skilled at acting less capable, less competent, or weaker than they really are. The reason this occurs is that experiences and messages have taught them to see themselves that way and to act accordingly. Both survivors and martyrs are victims.

Relationships That Build Victims

People learn to be or to act powerless by experiencing relationships that have either prepared them to be abused, or *not* prepared them to not be abused. We refer to these as "shame-based" relationships.

Shame is not to be confused with guilt. Let us remind you again that guilt is an emotional indication about wrong actions or attitudes. It is the flare that explodes in our conscience and says, "I did something wrong and I feel terrible about it." Guilt is a constructive signal, telling us to correct bad behaviors. Shame, on the other hand, is a destructive signal about you and your worth. It is the belief or mindset about yourself—that you are bad, defective or worthless as a person.

Shame-based relationships are relationships based on messages of shame: "You are so weak and defective that you are nothing without this relationship." Shame, then, is the glue that holds things together. It is the force that motivates people to refrain from certain behaviors and to do others.

Families, churches or any group of interrelated people who are shame-based send messages to their members that they are:

- Not loved and accepted.
- Not even lovable or acceptable.
- Only loved and accepted if, when, or because they perform well.
- Not capable, valuable, or worthwhile.
- Very alone, not really belonging anywhere, to anything, or with anyone.

An examination of the following seven characteristics of shame-based relationships will help explain how victims are built in these relationships.[1] We will give both the *dynamic* at work and the *effect* on the one who submits to this type of treatment.

1. Out-Loud Shaming

The dynamic: This is the "shame on you" that comes from name-calling, belittling, put-downs, comparing one person to another or asking, "What's wrong with you?" It is any message communicated out loud that says, "Something is wrong with you."

The effects: Negative view of self, even self-hatred; negative self-talk ("I'm no good, stupid, incapable."); shaming others.

2. Focus on Performance

The dynamic: How people act is more important than who they are or what is happening to them on the inside. Love and acceptance are earned by doing or not doing certain things. Living up to the standard is what earns acceptance, the result of which is acceptance of *behaviors*, not *people*. Or once the standard is reached, it is changed or moved. Kids can't be kids because children are imperfect, messy, loud and ask questions that sometimes perplex or embarrass, none of which is considered acceptable.

The effects: Perfectionism, or giving up without trying; doing only those things you are good at; cannot admit mistakes; procrastination; view of God as more concerned with how you act than who you are; cannot ask for help; cannot rest when tired; cannot have guilt-free fun; high need for the approval of others; sense of shame or self-righteousness; demanding of others, or you expect "nothing" from them; living a double life.

3. Manipulation

The dynamic: Relationships and behaviors are manipulated by very powerful *unspoken rules*. These rules are seldom, if ever, said out loud. In fact, when spoken out loud many of them sound ridiculous. No one says out loud, "What people think about us is more important than what is really happening." Yet the unspoken rules communicate these and other shaming messages.

The "can't-talk" rule keeps people quiet by labeling them as the problem if they notice and confront a problem. Because people feel

---

[1]For a more complete examination of shame and shame-based relationships, see *Tired of Trying to Measure Up*, by Jeff VanVonderen, Bethany House Publishers, 1989.

they cannot talk about an unspoken rule, they learn to talk in "code" to convey what they mean.

Coding is an example of verbal manipulation. When we "code," we say something in a crooked manner. Messages are sent through a verbal code that others are supposed to decode. "Oh, you don't have to go to all that trouble," actually means, "I'm embarrassed to ask for this treatment—but I like it!" "Don't you think it would be better this way?" means, "I want you to do it this way." People also code non-verbally with body language—by giving dirty looks, becoming loud or quiet, or leaving the room in a sullen or disconnected attitude.

Triangling is another way to act manipulative in relationships. This simply means to send a message to someone through another person instead of delivering it directly.

The effects: Great "radar"—the ability to pick up tension in situations and relationships; ability to decode the crooked messages of others; saying things in code instead of saying them straight; talking *about* people instead of *to* them; message-carrying for people; expecting others to know your code; difficulty trusting people; reading other meanings into what people say.

4. Idolatry

The dynamic: The "god" served by the shame-based relationship system is an impossible-to-please judge, obsessing on people's behaviors from a distance, whose mood is dependent on them. It is a god invented to enforce the performance standard and to keep the system intact. This is a false god, or idol. Anything you serve besides God, or anything from which you derive your sense of life, value and acceptance, is an idol. The false gods of the shame-based system are: appearance, or how things look; what people think; power-orientation.

The effects: Distorted image of God; high level of anxiety based on other people or external circumstances; people-pleasing; high need to control thoughts, feelings and behaviors of others in order to gain a sense of well-being.

5. Preoccupation With Fault and Blame

The dynamic: Since performance has so much power in these systems, much is brought to bear in order to control it. Reaction is swift and furious toward the one who fails to perform the way the system deems fit. People have to pay for their mistakes. Responsibility and accountability are not the issues here: Fault and blame are the issues. In the New Testament, the purpose of confessing a sin is to receive forgiveness and cleansing. The shame-based system wants a confession in order to know whom to shame—that is, whom to make feel so defective and humiliated that they won't act that way anymore. The effects: The sense that if something is wrong or someone is upset you must have caused it; a high need to be punished for or to pay for mistakes in order to feel good about yourself; defensive "skills" (blaming, rationalizing, minimizing, lying); critical of others; giving others the "third-degree"; need to be right; difficulty forgiving self; difficulty accepting grace and forgiveness from God.

6. Obscured Reality

The dynamic: In shame-based systems, members have to deny any thought, opinion or feeling that is different than those of people in authority. Anything that has the potential to shame those in authority is ignored or denied. People can't find out about life through normal trial-and-error learning because mistakes shame. Interaction with people and places outside the system threatens the order of things. The system defines reality. Consequently, you can't find out what "normal" is. Problems are denied, and therefore they remain.

The effects: Out-of-touch with feelings, needs, thoughts; ignoring your "radar" because you are being "too critical"; feel like no one else understands you; guessing at what is normal; threatened by opinions that differ from yours; afraid to take healthy risks; self-analytical; suspicious or afraid of others; narrow-minded; suffering stress-related illnesses; extreme forms of denial, even delusion.

7. Unbalanced Interrelatedness

The dynamic: Members of shame-based systems are either under-involved or over-involved with each other. Another word for under-involvement is *neglect*. Children of workaholics experience this because one or both parents are not there to teach about life. Consequently, rules take the place of people. There is no relationship structure in which to learn about behaviors and consequences. People find out about life alone and by accident. Another word for over-involvement is *enmeshment*. This is when there are no clear boundaries between people. Two lies govern: First, it is your responsibility to make sure everyone else is happy and well and you have the ability to achieve this. Second, everyone else is responsible to make sure *you* are happy and well and they are capable of doing so. Consequently, everyone is responsible for everyone else, while ironically no one is responsible for *himself or herself.*

The effects: Fear of being deserted; lack of self-discipline; rebelling against structure; high need for structure; a sense that if there is a problem, you have to solve it; feeling selfish for having needs; putting up boundaries that keep safe people away; continually letting unsafe people come close; difficulty saying no; allowing others to take advantage of you; feeling alone; possessive in relationships; feelings of guilt when you haven't done anything wrong; rescuing others from the consequences of their behaviors.

If you have come from shame-based relationships in which you were spiritually abused, you may hold to these or other unspoken rules:

- God rewards spirituality with material goods.
- "If I am spiritual enough, things won't affect me emotionally."
- "I can never say no to those in religious authority."
- Everyone in the ministry is called by God, is appropriate, and must be trusted.
- "God needs me to do ministry."
- "The existence of trouble in my life indicates a lack of faith."
- "Talking about problems will make God 'look bad.' "
- Unity means agreeing about everything.[2]

As you can see, shame-based relationships have significant effects upon those who have experienced them. The relational applications of these effects are far-reaching. As pertaining to spiritual systems, the application is clear: Shame-based relationships build on an emotional foundation that undermines relational honesty; hinders a maturing individual relationship with God; and fosters dependence upon another, who grows in power as a false leader, building an unhealthy system in which appearance is more important than reality. These systems victimize people and set them up to be trapped in future abusive relationships.

Conclusion

To this point, we have discussed the general symptoms of spiritual abuse. But not all families or churches or leaders who sometimes slip

---

[2]Stephen Arterburn and Jack Felton, *Toxic Faith* (Nashville, Tenn.: Oliver-Nelson Publishers, 1991).

into legalism, or who occasionally out of insecurity "pull rank," should be labeled as abusive.

We now direct your attention to common characteristics that identify the truly abusive system.

Just as spiritual abuse victims have a lot in common, so do the religious systems that perpetrate the abuse. When power is postured and religious performance legislated, watch out! When those who notice the problem become *the problem, beware!*

The truth is never the problem. Look now at the truth about spiritually abusive religious systems.

5

Identifying the Abusive System

There are certain characteristics that can be observed in all spiritually abusive systems. In the next two chapters, we will identify and describe seven that seem most common. This chapter will focus on *the unhealthy dynamics that dictate how people function within spiritually abusive systems.* In the following chapter, we will talk about *the dynamics that create walls around abusive systems,* making it difficult for people to get out.

Both dynamics are important to understand because, as with other abuses, it is common for spiritually abused people to move from one abusive system to another. Many do get up the courage to leave an abusive church but, lo and behold, in their next church they miss the signals or they talk themselves out of seeing the same dynamics that were present in the system from which they have just escaped.

Relationships between people in spiritually abusive systems are dictated by the following dynamics:

1. Power-Posturing

The first characteristic of an abusive religious system is what we call power-posturing. Power-posturing simply means that leaders spend a lot of time focused on their own authority and reminding others of it, as well. This is necessary because their spiritual authority isn't real—based on genuine godly character—it is postured.

Recently, a young couple told of attending a church where the pastor insisted that members treat what he says as if Christ himself had said it because, "In this flock, I'm the chief shepherd." If this pastor's spiritual authority were real, he would not have to demand that others notice it. Nor would he step into the idolatrous position he places himself in, assuming the place reserved for the King of Kings!

Matthew 7 says of Jesus: "When Jesus had finished [His] words, the multitudes were amazed at His teaching; for He was teaching them as one having authority, and not as their scribes" (vv. 28–29). While the scribes and Pharisees posed as authorities on the basis of their position, Jesus *had* authority, and people could tell. In his book, *Taking Our Cities for God*, John Dawson says, "The one who offers the most hope has the most authority."[1] Jesus offered us the greatest hope of all.

Those who are in positions of true leadership demonstrate authority, spiritual power, and credibility *by their lives and message*. If they don't, they are not truly leaders. The reason any of us is given spiritual authority is because God has led us through real-life experiences, by which He has revealed himself and His living Word to be true. Spiritual authority is seen in the man or woman who says, by his or her life, "God and His Word are true—I've proven them in the fibres of my being. I know there is hope in God!"

As Romans 13:1 says, "For there is no authority except from God." In Matthew 28:18 Jesus says, "All authority *has been given* to Me in heaven and on earth." Matthew 10:1 says, "And having summoned His twelve disciples, He *gave them* authority." Being hired or elected to a spiritual position, talking the loudest, or giving the most does not give someone authority. God does give it, and He does so for the purpose of coming underneath people in the body of Christ to build them, serve them, equip them and set them free to do God's agenda—which may or may not coincide with the agenda of the leadership.

No question, there are many leaders in the body of Christ whom people follow for the right reason—that is, because God has given them authority and they shepherd the flock. They set people free. Unfortunately, there are others who are elected leaders, but don't demonstrate any real authority to set people spiritually free. They spend a lot of energy posturing about how much authority they have and how much everyone else is supposed to submit to it. The fact that they are eager to place people *under* them—under their word, under their "authority"—is one easy-to-spot clue that they are operating in their *own* authority.

---

[1]John Dawson, *Taking Our Cities for God* (Strang Communications, 1989).

2. Performance Preoccupation

In abusive spiritual systems, power is postured and authority is legislated. Therefore, these systems are preoccupied with the performance of their members. *Obedience* and *submission* are two important words often used.

The following is an excerpt from a church newsletter, from the Pastor's personal column:

"Fallen from Grace"

Last Sunday, we fell below the 200 mark for the first time in 13 weeks. Our 200 + attendance mark has been stopped at 13. It happened, we fell from grace! . . . I would really like to see all of our folks join together for worship during these next four Sundays and help [the year] go out with a bang. We can make this truly a banner year at our church. We've had great attendance, great giving, great participation in all of our programs. Let's set the stage for a brand new decade by getting "graced up" again.

How did these people receive God's grace in the first place? By coming to church? By having 200 + people? How did they lose grace? By not having 200 people? What a distorted view of grace! Is he trying to get his people "graced up" or trying to get them to perform? Do we come to church to be encouraged about trusting Jesus, or to be pressed to try harder?

It's likely that this evangelical pastor would equate church attendance with obedience to Christ. But God teaches that He looks first upon the heart; God is concerned that we not do the right thing for all the wrong reasons. Yes, obedience to God is not negotiable. Yet the way to tell if someone is doing the right thing for the wrong reason is if they are keeping track of it. Let's say that another way. If obedience and service is flowing out of you as a result of your dependence on God alone, you won't keep track of it with an eye toward reward, you'll just do it. But if you're preoccupied with whether you've done enough to please God, then you're not looking at Him, you're looking at your own works. And you're also concerned about who else might be looking at you, evaluating you. Why would anyone keep track of their "godly" behavior unless they were trying to earn spiritual points because of it?

Consider the sad example of one church, which started out with a ministry that provided a valuable service to people in the community. Unfortunately, those who served in that ministry were required to go before the leadership and document how they spent every minute of every day. They were evaluated based upon whether they used their time wisely, "the way God wants you to use it." Most were confronted for not reading their Bible enough—and the leadership decided what "enough" was. They were also confronted for spending 15 minutes instead of 10 when taking a bath. After all, they should have been reading the Bible during that extra five minutes—meaning that in this system the leadership also decided what was the right "spiritual" amount of time to bathe. This system does not foster holiness or obedience to God, it merely accommodates the leaders' sick interpretation of spirituality and their need for control.

Are obedience and submission important? Without question. This can be seen in Romans 13:1: "Let every person be in subjection to the governing authorities." And 1 Peter 5:5 says, "Be subject to your elders." Hebrews 13:17 also says, emphatically, "Obey your leaders, and submit to them." To bring balance, however, we must add to these verses an equally important passage. Consider the words of Peter and the other apostles in Acts 5:29: "We must obey God rather than men." Notice that Peter is saying this to the religious leaders he was disobeying. Out of context, obedience to leaders looks like good theology. Add the larger context, and you will see that *it is only appropriate to obey and submit to leadership when their authority is from God and their stance is consistent with His.*

For many reasons, followers sometimes obey or follow orders to avoid being shamed, to gain someone's approval, or to keep their spiritual status or church position intact. This is not true obedience or submission; it is compliant self-seeking. When behavior is simply legislated from the outside, instead of coming from a heart that loves God, it cannot be called obedience. It is merely weak compliance with some form of external pressure.

In Romans 12:2 Paul says, "Do not be conformed to this world, but be transformed by the renewing of your mind." Don't be conformed but be *transformed.* Now the word *conformed* means "squeezed from the outside in." So Paul is saying, "Don't be squeezed." In a performance-focused church or family, that verse might be applied like this: "Our church or leader is right; we have a truer, purer 'word' from God than others. Therefore, we must adhere to our formula or brand of Christianity as hard and fast as possible—so we won't become like those *out there* who don't think as we do. If I do not live up to all I've been taught here, I will be letting God down." This orientation squeezes people from the outside in. They are not transformed, they are conformed.

Transformation is an inside-out job; not outside-in. Don't allow yourself to be squeezed. Be transformed!

3. Unspoken Rules

In abusive spiritual systems, people's lives are controlled from the outside in by rules, spoken and unspoken. Unspoken rules are those that govern unhealthy churches or families but are not said out loud. Because they are not said out loud, you don't find out that they're there until you break them.

For instance, no one at a church gathering would ever say out loud, "You know we must never disagree with the pastor on his sermons—and if you do you will never be trusted and never be allowed to minister in any capacity in this church." In this case, the unspoken rule is: Do not disagree with the church authorities—especially the pastor—or your loyalty will be suspect. Rules like this remain unspoken because examining them in the light of mature dialogue would instantly reveal how illogical, unhealthy and anti-Christian they are. So silence becomes the fortress wall of protection, shielding the pastor's power position from scrutiny or challenge.

If you did disagree openly or publicly, you would break the silence—and you would quite likely be punished. You would unwittingly discover that there is a rule, even though it's not spoken. When you find unspoken rules by breaking them unintentionally, you will then suffer one of two consequences: either *neglect* (being ignored, overlooked, shunned) or *aggressive legalism* (questioned, openly censured, asked to leave—in extreme cases cursed).

Unspoken rules have an incredible amount of power. Perhaps you are living under the effects of several right now. Let's take a test.

Did you come from a religious background where it was taught that the written rule, the Bible, has the final say? "The Bible is the final authority" was the spoken rule. In that church or family was there also an unwritten and unspoken rule that said, "It is better to be nice than to be honest"? Now, the written rule—the Bible—says in Ephesians 4:25: "Therefore, laying aside falsehood, speak truth, each one of you, with his neighbor, for we are members of one another."

Now we have a conflict. The written rule says one thing, the unwritten rule says another. Now here is the test. For those who came from a system where both rules were in operation, which rule won most often? Was honesty suppressed, repressed, or even oppressed? In spiritually abusive families and churches, where people insist that they stand on the authority of Scripture, not even Scripture is as powerful as the unwritten rules.

The "Can't Talk" Rule

The most powerful of all unspoken rules in the abusive system is what we have already termed the "can't-talk" rule. The "can't-talk" has this thinking behind it: "The real problem cannot be exposed because then it would have to be dealt with and things would have to change; so it must be protected behind walls of silence (neglect) or by assault (legalistic attack). If you speak about the problem out loud, *you are the problem*. In some way you must be silenced or eliminated." Those who do speak out are most often told, "We didn't have all these problems until you started shooting your mouth off. Everything was fine before you started stirring things up." Or else, to make it sound really spiritual, "You were angry—you didn't confront the matter in a 'loving' way. So it proves you weren't handling the matter in a mature, Christian manner." In either case, the problem remains.

The truth is, when people talk about problems out loud they don't *cause* them, they simply *expose* them.

In abusive spiritual systems, there exists a "pretend peace"—what Jeremiah decried, saying, "The prophets say 'peace, peace' when there is none." If what unites us is our pretending to agree, even though we don't agree, then we have nothing more than pretend peace and unity, with undercurrents of tension and backbiting. This is far from "preserving unity and peace in the Holy Spirit," which is to be the hallmark of healthy Christian churches. That is to say, any topic should be open for discussion, and on some points we may *agree to disagree* and to continue open dialogue on the subject, both parties willing; or we may both agree to suspend discussion for a time if it raises tension. The important point is that both parties be involved in forming the agreement. If what unites us truly is the Holy Spirit and love for one another, then it is possible to disagree and it will not destroy our unity.

The "can't-talk" rule, however, blames the person who talks, and the ensuing punishments pressure questioners into silence.

Here is another test. Susan is being counseled by John, a Christian counselor and leader in the church. John makes aggressive sexual advances toward Susan after a counseling session one afternoon. Susan reports the incident to the church leaders and the secular authorities. John gets in trouble and is taken before courts and boards and committees. Why did John get in trouble?

Was it because Susan exposed him? No. John got into trouble

because his advances were inappropriate and illegal. What he might do, however, is somehow communicate to her (and maybe enlist the help of the pastor and other people in the church) that the reason why he's in so much trouble is because Susan spoke up.

Sadly, there are many women like Susan who suffer spiritual abuse when they are called "unsubmissive," "too strong," "disloyal," or "a Jezebel" for exposing abusive Christian male leaders, or even for questioning them. Too many churches communicate this kind of shaming message: "The problem is not that your boundaries were crossed and violated, the problem is that you talked. If you would not have made such a big deal, everything would still be fine." If a person accepts that message, they *will* stop talking.

The real problem, however, is that if a Christian who feels violated stops talking, then the perpetrator will never be held accountable for his behavior. And the victim will have to "freeze up" the pain and anger of being spiritually abused.

Though some in authority would love to never be questioned or opposed, the fact of the matter is that such a system is a trap and a downfall for any leader. If noticing problems is labeled disloyalty, lack of submission, divisiveness, and a challenge to authority, then there is only a facade of peace and unity. It is impossible for wounds to be healed, and abuse will one day escalate. If authorities are not accountable, then you have built a system that is in opposition to the freedom that is in Christ. You are ignoring James 3:1, which says, "Let not many of you become teachers, my brethren, knowing that as such we shall incur a stricter judgment."

Leaders are *more* accountable because of their position of authority—not less accountable. Why? Because if you are a leader people are following you, behaving the way you do. You are spiritually reproducing after your own kind. What are *you* reproducing?

4. Lack of Balance

The fourth characteristic of a spiritually abusive system is an unbalanced approach to living out the truth of the Christian life. This shows itself in two extremes:

Extreme Objectivism

The first extreme is an empirical approach to life, which elevates *objective truth* to the exclusion of *valid subjective experience*. This is seen in religious systems where even though the Holy Spirit's work might be acknowledged theologically, on a practical level it would be suspect, or denied.

This approach to spirituality creates a system in which authority is based upon the level of education and intellectual capacity alone, rather than on intimacy with God, obedience and sensitivity to His Spirit. This kind of system is in opposition to Scripture and the Spirit of God. Consider Acts 4:13: "Now as [the religious leaders] observed the confidence of Peter and John, and understood that they were uneducated and untrained men, they were marveling, and began to recognize them as having been with Jesus." Peter and John's confidence and authority come from the fact that they had been with Jesus, and they were "filled with the Holy Spirit" (Acts 4:8).

The objective spiritual system limits God to act only in those ways that we can explain, prove, or experience. It puts God in a box. We are left with a Trinity of God the Father, God the Son, and God *the Holy Bible*—as if understanding and memorizing Scripture is the only way to hear from God. We are relegated to songs that commemorate how God used to do things. We no longer worship the great I Am, but the great "I Was."

Extreme Subjectivism

The other manifestation of lack of balance is seen in an extremely subjective approach to the Christian life. What is true is decided on the basis of feelings and experiences, giving more weight to them than to what the Bible declares. In this system, people can't know or understand truths (even if they really do understand or know them) until the leaders "receive them by spiritual revelation from the Lord" and "impart" them to the people.

In such systems, it is more important to act according to the word of a leader who has "a word" for you than to act according to what you know to be true from Scripture, or simply from your spiritual growth-history.

As an aside, our personal belief is that "words of wisdom" and "words of knowledge" can come from God through spiritually sensitive men and women today. But these "words" do not automatically carry the same authoritative weight as those of Paul, Peter, James or John— one of those whose words are in our Bible and are the very Word of God. The only way to be *absolutely* certain that a word from the Lord is for you is if it's *the* Word of the Lord, that is, Scripture. Even in this, we are never to use Scriptures to manipulate people. ("I was reading about Ananias and Saphira and you came to mind. Are you sure you're giving enough to the church?") The fact that someone reads the actual Word of God to you does not necessarily mean that they have a word from the Lord for you.

A directive, guiding, or correcting word from the Lord, whether from Scripture or in the form of a spiritual gift, will be confirmed by the Holy Spirit, who lives in you. Until He does confirm it, do not receive it as a word from the Lord, even if it comes from an elder or a pastor. Even further, we believe it is dishonest— even dangerous—simply to receive and act upon a spiritual directive because you are "supposed to be submissive," or because someone is "in authority." In the end, God is the One before whom we must all stand, the One to whom we must answer.

As with the extreme objective approach, Christians who are highly subjective also have a view of education—most often, that education is bad or unnecessary. There is almost a pride in *not* being educated, and a disdain for those who are. Everything that is needed is taught by the Holy Spirit. ("After all, Peter and Timothy didn't go to college or seminary. . . .")

The truth is that Peter *did* go to seminary. Both objective truth and subjective experience were given to him by Jesus. Timothy's seminary was Paul. That is because, in their day, people were taught through the Rabbinic method of teaching. This meant living with and experiencing life with a spiritual mentor. Peter's discipleship lasted three years. Even after Timothy got into the ministry he continued "seminary" through the mail, if you will. Remember that Paul wrote to Timothy in 2 Timothy 2:15, "Be diligent to present yourself approved to God as a workman who does not need to be ashamed, handling accurately the word of truth." The familiar King James Version says, "Study to show yourself approved. . . ."

It is important to study the Word of God. And it is good, not bad, to acquire mental tools to handle God's Word accurately.

Beware of those who put a spiritual premium on not being educated, or of being educated only at certain schools. In the name of some "higher enlightenment" by the Holy Spirit, you may be withering under a teacher with a limited reality who won't be taught by anyone else.

In the next chapter we will examine those characteristics of spiritually abusive systems that make it difficult for people to leave.

People within spiritually abusive systems are wounded and tired. The previous chapter helped explain why. Now we would like to examine why many find it difficult or impossible to leave, even after the abuse is recognized.

6

When You Cannot Leave

In the field of astronomy there is a phenomenon called a "black hole." A black hole is a star whose mass got so incredibly dense that it actually "imploded"—that is, instead of exploding *outward* it exploded *inward*. Now its gravity has grown so strong that it prevents even light from leaving. Hence, the term "black hole."

As we've noted, certain characteristics of spiritually abusive systems make it immensely difficult for people caught up in them to leave. Because of the focus on religious performance, things look good to those on the outside. This system acts like a "spiritual magnet" pulling in people from the outside. Inside, however, the system acts like a black hole with spiritual gravity so strong it is very hard for people to get out. In fact, as you've already seen with the "can't-talk" rule, even information about what is going on within the system can't get out. If you talk to anyone, you are treated as if *you* are the problem. The following characteristics are what make these abusive spiritual systems so difficult to escape.

5. Paranoia

In the church or family that is spiritually abusive, there is a sense, spoken or unspoken, that "others will not understand what we're all about, so let's not let them know—that way they won't be able to ridicule or persecute us." There is an assumption that (1) what we say, know, or do is a result of our being more enlightened than others; (2) others will not understand unless they become one of us; and (3) others will respond negatively.

In a place where authority is grasped and legislated, not simply demonstrated, persecution sensitivity builds a case for keeping everything within the system. Why? Because of the evil, dangerous, or unspiritual people outside of the system who are trying to weaken or destroy "us." This mentality builds a strong wall or bunker around the abusive system, isolates the abusers from scrutiny and accountability, and makes it more difficult for people to leave—because they will then be outsiders too. While it is true that there is a world of evil outside of the system, there is also good out there. But people are misled into thinking that the *only* safety is in the system.

Ironically, Jesus and Paul both warned that one of the worst dangers to the flock was from wolves *in the house* (Matthew 10:16; Acts 20:29–30).

Not long ago, we heard about a ministry in the western U.S. that began with quite an exceptional reputation. At some point, however, the leader started doing things that were questionable, even illegal and immoral. A newspaper started asking questions and his escapades were called into question. This man ended up having a lawsuit filed against him for being sexually inappropriate. He settled out of court, so the problem would disappear—and then he disappeared.

During the time he was being scrutinized, though, his response was interesting—if not sad. Whenever the local paper came out with an article questioning or exposing his activities, he would issue a newsletter that echoed the same rhetoric: "We must be getting really close to what God wants us to do, because Satan has renewed his attacks against us through the evil secular media!" We believe that because no one within the religious system would speak the truth, God used the media to reveal the tragic facts about this man's life.

This is one example of paranoia, or focusing on an external enemy to keep from answering legitimate questions.

Keeping People Wounded

Not only does this spiritualized paranoia make it hard to leave the system, it prevents people from getting the help they need.

"Do you want to have no fear of authority?" Paul asks in Romans 13:3. "Then do what is good." He does not tell us to hide the problem.

How sad when we hear that a pastor has covered up child abuse in one of his church families because of distrusting the "evil, secular, social service system." It's true, the welfare department does not know about God's grace and love—but neither do the Christian parents who are abusing their children. What the social services people *do* know is how to help someone who is being abused. And they know how to hold perpetrators of abuse accountable for their behavior. A child abuser is breaking the law, and God uses the legal system as "an avenger who brings wrath upon the one who practices evil" (Romans 13:4).

Another example of spiritual paranoia is the way many Christians respond to Alcoholics Anonymous and other self-help groups. AA is the most readily available, custom-made support group for people who need support to quit drinking. It does not promise to bring people to Jesus (and so it should not be held accountable to do what it does not promise to do). It does, however, help people get sober. Yet, many Christians won't go to or refer others to AA because it does not acknowledge Jesus Christ as Savior and Lord.

True, AA does not exist primarily to help people in their Christian walk (although if they were not drunk their Christian walk would no doubt improve). And true, they refer to a "higher power" and "God, as you understand Him." But which one of us does not have a relationship with God *as we understand Him?* AA allows people with incredibly negative images of God to begin to seek Him again without having to master a lot of theology to do so. It's also possible that AA has sent many more people to the church than the church has sent to AA.

Let's never forget that one of our main functions in guiding God's flock is to find spiritual help for hurting people—even if it means submitting to someone who has expertise in an area where we have little or no wisdom.

As a final and admittedly extreme case of containing wounded Christians in an abusive system through fear, we'd like to share the most bizarre example we have ever encountered. It illustrates, if nothing else, how far off-balance a self-contained spiritual system can become.

A couple of years ago, on two separate occasions, we spoke with two different couples who had recently left the same church. Neither couple knew that we had seen the other couple from their former church, nor were they told. While each couple reported similar reasons for leaving, their stories were not exactly the same. There was one situation that they reported identically, though—and it was chilling.

Many others had recently become upset and left this same church, funneling into other churches in the area. Both couples reported that their former pastor and his wife were so extremely concerned about what was being said about them in the other churches that they engaged in, and taught others to engage in, the practice of *astral projection*—"soul travel"—so they could invisibly enter the homes of dissident flock members to listen in on them and make sure they weren't "gossiping" about the pastor. The thought of such extreme paranoia and what it can do under spiritual guises needs to stand as a warning.

6. Misplaced Loyalty

Recently, we heard of a Christian organization that makes its youth workers sign a "loyalty statement." In it, they promise that if they ever leave the organization they won't minister to youth in that area for a period of so many years.

We have to ask: Whose kingdom are we building? If we are all building God's kingdom, why do we have to sign a loyalty oath, promising not to build next door to each other?

The next characteristic of spiritually abusive systems is that a misplaced sense of loyalty is fostered and even demanded. We're not talking about loyalty to Christ, but about loyalty to a given organization, church, or leader.

Once again, because authority is assumed or legislated (and therefore not real), *following* must be legislated as well. A common way this is accomplished is by setting up a system where disloyalty to or disagreement with the leadership is construed as the same thing as disobeying God. Questioning leaders is equal to questioning God. After all, the leader is the authority, and authority is always right. This causes people to misplace their loyalty in a leader, a church, or an organization. Once again, this makes the wall around the system thicker and makes it more difficult to leave.

"We Alone Are Right"

There are three factors that come into play here, adding up to misplaced loyalty. First, leadership projects a "we alone are right" mentality, which permeates the system. Members must remain in the system if they want to be "safe," or to stay "on good terms" with God, or not to be viewed as wrong or "backslidden."

I (Jeff speaking) used to work at a substance-abuse treatment center. At times, members of the staff would ask to go to the University of Minnesota or Hazelden for a continuing education experience and some new, fresh ideas on how to treat the addicted. We were told, "We can teach you all that you need to know here. In fact, we can do it better than either of those two places. We know more than they do." If someone decided to go anyway, they were "punished" when they returned by receiving the silent treatment, or by having their new insights ridiculed.

In contrast to the "we-alone-are-right" mentality, I'll share a parallel I like to use with the members of our church. Let's say someone came to me and said, "I don't agree with what you're teaching and I can't support this church." I would ask what the disagreement was (to clarify), and if indeed we did disagree, then I would simply tell them, "You need to be in a place where you can open up your heart and receive what God has to give. If this church can't do that for you, then you should feel good about finding a place where you feel a better fit. If it doesn't work out and you want to come back, come back. But go where God tells you to go. You and the Holy Spirit have to figure that one out." I would not ascribe disloyalty or lack of spirituality to someone who left our church.

Scare Tactics

The second factor that brings about misplaced loyalty is the use of "scare tactics." We've already seen some of this in the paranoia described in the last section. Scare tactics are more serious. This is more than just the risk of being polluted by the world.

Not long ago a Christian man made it clear to us that he had separated himself from the world by not fellowshiping with "the infidels." As we talked, we learned that his definition of "infidel" was not limited to non-Christians. It also included Christians from other denominations, certain Christians from his own denomination, and even Christians from his own church who didn't think as he did. In fact, we were dismayed to learn that we were also considered "infidels" because we failed to agree with him.

We have counseled many Christians who, after deciding to leave their church, were told horrifying things. "God is going to withdraw His Spirit from you and your family." "God will destroy your business." "Without our protection, Satan will get your children." "You and your family will come under a curse." This is spiritual blackmail and it's abuse. And it does cause people to stay in abusive places.

Humiliation

The third method of calling forth misplaced loyalty is the threat of humiliation. This is done by publicly shaming, exposing, or threatening to remove people from the group.

Unquestionably, there is a place for appropriate church discipline (which we will discuss later). In the abusive system, it is the *fear* of being exposed, humiliated or removed that insures your proper allegiance, and insulates those in authority. You can be "exposed" for asking too many questions, for disobeying the unspoken rules, or for disagreeing with authority. People are made public examples in order to send a message to those who remain. Others have phone campaigns launched against them, to warn their friends and others in the group about how "dangerous" they are.

One of several things usually happens after such pressures are employed. First, people stay and shut up. Second, they are eventually driven away because they end up isolated and spiritually starved to death. Third, they finally get up and say, "Fine, I am leaving because this is abusive and I disagree."

Many people have reported a curious thing after having taken such a stand. Although many in the system wanted them to leave when they did, they received calls and correspondence asking them to come back again. This is so confusing that some people actually go back.

7. Secretive

When you see people in a religious system being secretive—*watch out*. People don't hide what is appropriate; they hide what is inappropriate.

One reason spiritually abusive families and churches are secretive is because they are so image conscious. People in these systems can't even live up to their own performance standards, so they have to hide what is real. Some believe they must do this in order to protect God's good name. So how things look and what others think becomes more important than what's real. They become God's "public relations agents." The truth is, He's not hiring anyone for this position.

Another reason for secrecy in a church is that the leadership has a condescending, negative view of the laity. This results in conspiracies on the leadership level. They tell themselves, "People are not mature enough to handle truth." This is patronizing, at best. Conspiracies also develop among the lay people. Since it is not all right to notice or talk about problems, people form conspiracies behind closed doors and over the telephone as they try to solve things informally. But since they have no authority, they solve, and solve, and solve—but nothing really gets solved. And all the while, building God's true kingdom is put on hold.

When I (Jeff speaking) was working in that treatment center, there was a conspiracy among the staff concerning problems with the management. Instead of confronting issues (knowing that if we did we were in for trouble), we would meet together behind closed doors. Small groups of staff members solved and solved agency issues with each other, but it never did any good. It also got to the point where we spent more time solving the problems of the agency behind closed doors than we did ministering to people who were our needy clients.

Conclusion

When these characteristics exist in a church or Christian family system, the result will be spiritual abuse. It will be a closed system, with rigid boundaries that prevent people from leaving. There will be the perception of a lot of evil on the outside, to keep people in, and there will be a lot of power postured on the inside to compel you to perform. There will also be tired, wounded people who feel that they are either unspiritual or crazy. And they will have major problems relating to God from the heart.

In addition, people who live in these systems can wind up totally ill-equipped for life. When they leave, for whatever reason, they may be blown around like dry leaves, or easily drawn into other abusive systems.

How is this possible? How could someone who loves God decide to shun Him? And how could someone who has once been abused in a spiritual setting jump into the arms of further abuse?

We believe one answer lies in the abusive system's use—or misuse—of Scripture. This is a most serious problem, which bears close examination.

Used rightly, the Word of God is a sword, exposing motives of the heart, and a lamp, lighting the way for those who follow God. Misused, it can become nothing more than a club in the hands of those who equate pretending with obedience and silence with peace. Let's look at the difference.

7

Abuse and Scripture

Not long ago I (Jeff speaking) taught a course at a seminary on how shame-based issues affect churches and families. After presenting a session on spiritual abuse, a woman approached me at the podium.

"I just can't bring myself to read the Bible anymore," she blurted. "I feel sad because God's Word used to be important to me. But now every time I try to read it I actually get an upset stomach."

After we talked a little more I discovered that she had been horribly abused with God's Word. Every time something happened to her or to anyone in her immediate family, she was referred to Scriptures about "supernatural faith." And she was told that if she'd been praying, "doing spiritual warfare," these attacks would not be getting through and harming her family.

"I guess I'm the problem, really. I don't have enough faith. I'm a weak Christian," she concluded. The anticipation of getting bad spiritual news was so great that she could no longer bring herself to read the Bible at all.

In Titus 1, Paul says that leaders in the church must be diligent in the sound teaching of God's Word:

> Hold fast the faithful word . . . for there are many rebellious men, empty talkers and deceivers, especially those of the circumcision, who must be silenced because they are upsetting whole families, teaching things they should not teach, for the sake of sordid gain. (vv. 9–11)

This passage opens to us the additional problem of placing heavy performance weights upon struggling people by means of misusing or abusing Scripture.

Instead of using the Word as a sword to pierce through to the thoughts and motives of their own hearts, many spiritual leaders have used it as a stick to drive others, for a variety of reasons: to keep others from holding them accountable; to protect their image; to uphold a doctrine they have based a whole ministry upon; to keep funds coming in; to build religious kingdoms in order to bolster their own spiritual self-esteem. In other words, it's possible that some leaders teach the Word for personal gain, not to heal and to free.

Setting the Stage

Three main factors operate in a spiritually abusive system that comprise the "soil" out of which scriptural abuse can grow. They are: *mindset, motive,* and *method.* A look at each of these will help you understand how they create an environment where people are scripturally abused.

The first factor is the *mindset* people have about themselves and Scripture. In a spiritually abusive system, the mindset of the people is that they have little or no capacity to discern God's Word themselves. Their view of Scripture is that of a book of rules, designed to cause behaviors that are pleasing to God, or designed to elicit a desired response from God. In other words, for them, the Bible is not a book that guides us into character transformation so we can be transformed into the likeness of Christ; it is a book about "techniques" for performing right so that we can get corresponding blessing out of God. Spirituality is replaced by manipulation.

As a result, these people view their leaders as those who have the last word on the meaning and purpose of God's Word because the leaders have (or say they have) success at *doing* and *receiving.* The mindset of the leaders—about themselves, Scripture, and their followers—is that they have "broken through" to some higher level of spiritual achievement, so they have "earned" the right to lead.

Please note that it is the "achievement" of the leaders that sets the performance standard of the flock. In some settings, it may be evangelizing or witnessing, or discipling young Christians, or claiming victories by faith, or starting home cell groups—whatever the personality of the leadership dictates. In other words, doing more of the prescribed behavior is the goal, *not* inner transformation into the likeness of Jesus. Those who do more of that behavior are rewarded; those who don't are ignored or counseled to do so; and those who are hurting are told that it is the answer to most or all of their maladies. This leads to the second factor.

In a spiritually abusive system, leaders "power posture" through the use of Scripture. The *motive* is to cause religious performance on the part of the people in order to meet the needs of the leaders, to "prove" that they and their theology are right. Again, the motive is not to "feed" the souls of the flock, nor to assist God in achieving whatever He wants in a person's life.

In addition to burning people out, pressuring people to "live up to" Scripture leads to a distorted perception of God. He becomes one who is created in the image of the leaders. This is not about helping people gain a deeper understanding of God through the Word, in all its multi-faceted beauty. In fact, a deeper understanding of Scripture on the part of the people would probably expose the whole abusive situation.

The third factor is the *method* used to study and apply the truth of Scripture. In a spiritually abusive system, Scripture is employed to prove or to bolster the agenda of the person using it. This is called "proof-texting." Proof-texting occurs when someone has a point he wants to prove. So he finds a verse to do so, even if it means stretching or ignoring the original issue about which the verse was written or the context in which the verse is found.

Because this is the method the leaders use, it is the method the followers learn to use. Consequently, there is little if any opportunity to become capable of "rightly dividing the word of truth."

In order to minimize the possibility of misusing Scripture, it is helpful to ask several questions about any particular text. To whom was it written? What kinds of problems or issues were facing the people being addressed? What did it mean to the original hearers? Is this a timeless truth, or a specific instruction for a specific situation? Sometimes, even a brief look at the context of the passage being studied would reveal that the point someone is trying to "prove" by the text is completely different than the original intention of the writer.

We have talked to many people who have experienced scriptural abuse at the hands of spiritual leaders and others in churches and families. To share the extent of this abuse would take a book in itself. In this chapter we'll look at some specific examples in a few categories of life in which scriptural abuse takes place. But first we need to examine a broader misuse of Scripture from which a good deal of scriptural abuse stems. It concerns the Law of God, and the various other laws of God found throughout Scripture.[1]

---

[1]The Ten Commandments given to Moses (Exodus 20:3–17; Deuteronomy 5:6–21) summarize God's Law—His requirements for humanity. Jesus further summarized God's Law as requiring perfect love for God and for one's neighbor (Matthew 22:35–40).

Misusing God's Law

This kind of scriptural abuse represents a mindset that actually casts its shadow over all forms of scriptural abuse. It is rooted in one of two misunderstandings concerning the purpose for which God gave His Law.

First, there are many religious people who believe that a right relationship with God can be attained through performance of the Law. Yet Paul says in Galatians 2:16, "Knowing that a man is not justified by the works of the Law but through faith in Christ Jesus . . . since by the works of the Law shall no flesh be justified." Second, there are many Christians who believe that God gave His Law to provide a way to live victoriously, to receive blessing.

God did not give the Law so that people could become right with Him based upon their lawful behaviors. Neither are lawful behaviors the way to remain right with God. Right relationship with God is a settled gift because of what God did through Christ. You can't earn it. You can only have it for free.

Why Did God Give the Law?

There are three reasons why God gave the Law. First, He gave the Law so that we could see that we have sinned. God's standard is like a mirror that shows us our performance has fallen short of God's expectation. Romans 3:20 says, ". . . through the law [God's standard] comes the knowledge of sin [not living up to the standard]." It is a good thing to realize that you have missed the mark.

The second purpose of the Law is to convince us that we are helpless, through our own efforts, to hit the mark. Romans 11:32 says, "God has consigned all men to disobedience" (AMP). The Greek word for "consigned" means "to be locked up," as in prison. God's Law was not given as a means to peace with God. Neither is it to challenge us to live holy lives. It was given to show us that peace with God and holy lives are absolutely unattainable through self-effort. God's Law imprisons and defines us as persons who are in a state of missing the mark.

The third purpose of the Law is to bring us into a *grace-full* relationship with God on the basis of His own work of grace through Christ. Complete Romans 11:32 and you will see what I mean: "God has consigned all men to disobedience, *that He may have mercy upon all.*" God offers peace and right standing with himself as a gift at His own expense! Once this is accomplished, the purpose of the Law has been fulfilled. Romans 10:4 says, "For Christ is the end of the law for righteousness to everyone who believes."

This is made even more clear by Paul in Galatians 3:

> But before faith came, we were kept in custody under the law, being shut up [imprisoned] to the faith which was later to be revealed. Therefore the Law has become our tutor to lead us to Christ, that we may be justified by faith. But now that faith has come, we are no longer under a tutor. (vv. 23–25)

"Tutor" does not fully portray the job of the Law conveyed in this verse. Some translations use the words *teacher* or *schoolmaster*, which are even more unfortunate renderings of the word. The Greek word for "tutor" is *paidagogos*, which means "child disciplinarian." This person was hired by parents to escort their children to school. Whenever a child would veer from the path, the "tutor" would hit the child with a long stick. The kids were literally driven to school like cattle. Once at the school, however, where the real schoolmaster was, the job of the *paidagogos* was over. The tutor's job was to lead a child to the true place of learning. Just as the *paidagogos* would keep children on the right path and "drive" them to school, the Law acts as our "tutor" to drive us to Christ. As we wander off the path, the Law explicitly reminds us that we don't measure up to God's standard. It "beats" us back onto the path that leads us to a right relationship with Christ.

Once we are in a relationship with Christ, the child-disciplinarian is out of a job. Now that faith has come, we are no longer under the tutorship of the Law. If, however, you have returned or have been placed back under the Law—any law—as a means to live the Christian life, then you will eventually feel as tired and beat up as you should. Trying harder is the incorrect response to spiritual rules and will result in either self-righteousness or more tiredness. The correct response is to rest again in the performance of Christ, on the Cross for life, and through His Spirit for living.

Romans 7:4 says that something has happened in order for us to be able to bear fruit for God. "You also were made to die to the Law . . . that you might be joined to another, to Him who was raised from the dead." You will notice from the verse that we don't produce the fruit, we simply bear fruit that God produces. And if you've been spiritually abused, you may have noticed that spiritually abusive leaders attempt to get people to produce fruit. And the primary way they do this is by putting people back under Law, from which Christ died to free us.

Learning to "Do" Christianity

When I first became a Christian (Jeff speaking), I went to a week-long conference designed to teach me how to live the Christian life. The speaker presented us with list after list of "spiritual" things to do and ways to do them. When I went home, I noticed that I felt really bad about myself. And I figured that God felt pretty bad about me too. I was guilty and ashamed.

Since then, I have thought a lot about what happens at conferences like that. One thing that bothers me is that many verses used in the teaching are taken totally out of context. But then, since the goal of this kind of approach to the Christian life is to get certain behaviors, proof-texting is deemed perfectly acceptable.

I've also come to some conclusions. First, I don't think it is possible to leave a "Christian formula seminar" with a clean conscience. Under the banner of being a tutor to lead us to Christ, more often they cause people to become almost totally self-occupied. And when we look at ourselves we always fall short. I suppose that a person could scrutinize how they behave as a Christian and come out guilt-free. Unfortunately, this is called *self-righteousness*.

I also think that these kinds of seminars lead people to live the Christian life for the wrong reason. Self-occupied people who leave a formula seminar with a dirty conscience and a list of things to do attempt to live out the Christian life in order to clean up their conscience.

But consider this. In 1 Timothy 1, Paul writes, "But the goal of our instruction is love from a pure heart and a good conscience and sincere faith" (v. 5). In this passage Paul says that *the goal of his teaching is love which flows out of a clean conscience*—that is, a heart that is true and a faith that is real. Where do these things come from? From how well we do the list? From how we live our lives? No.

Look further, at Hebrews 10:

> Since therefore, brethren, we have confidence to enter the holy place by the blood of Jesus, by a new and living way which He inaugurated for us through the veil, that is, His flesh, and since we have a great priest over the house of God, let us draw near with *a sincere heart in full assurance of faith, having our hearts sprinkled clean from an evil conscience* and our bodies

washed with pure water. (vv. 19–22, italics added)

A clean conscience and pure heart are never possible on the basis of religious behaviors. And besides, they are already ours because of Jesus.

In 1 Timothy 1, Paul also says, "For some men, straying from these things, have turned aside to fruitless discussion, wanting to be teachers of the Law, even though they do not understand either what they are saying or the matters about which they make confident assertions" (vv. 6–7). It sounds as though there were "Christian formula seminars" in the first century, too.

Now with these thoughts on the appropriate and inappropriate use of the Law as background, let's look at some specific ways Scripture is misused as we have seen in the lives of people we have counseled. The verses used are representative, not exhaustive. To clarify before we begin, we are not saying to disregard these verses. They are important and useful, and we all must reckon with them. Yet they have at times been used in an abusive way.

Self-Denial

- *1 Corinthians 15:31*—"I die daily."

We have seen many people who have taken on the burden of trying to die daily. They become preoccupied with themselves, always looking to see if something needs to be denied or fixed. They are constantly trying hard not to *feel*, to *notice*, or to *want*.

In the context of 1 Corinthians 15, Paul is making a case for the dead being raised. In fact, it is because of his confidence in being raised from the dead that he feels totally free to put himself at risk for the sake of the gospel. In truth, he is at such constant physical risk he says, "I die daily." Look also at Galatians 2:20 and you will see that the old, dead "I" that Paul refers to has been put to death with Christ. The new, full-of-the-life-of-Christ "I" now lives on the basis of hanging on to Jesus, not by trying hard to do a list of religious behaviors.

- *Matthew 16:24*—"Then Jesus said to His disciples, 'If anyone wishes to come after Me, let him deny himself, and take up his cross, and follow Me.' "

This verse, like 1 Corinthians 15:31, has been misused in order to place a performance weight on people in the name of self-denial. In addition, "taking up the cross" in an abusive system usually turns out to be an attempt to get followers to take up the agenda of the leadership.

What we ought to be concerned about is directing people to the source of life, which comes from rest in the presence of God. The Christian life does not begin or continue with the kind of self-denial that calls for doing a lot of Christian behaviors in order to check "humility" off the list. Self-denial *is* crucial—so essential, in fact, that in order to have life we must deny that there is anything we ourselves can do to get it. It is only available on the basis of the cross of Christ. If *that* cross is not our "cross," if our own cross (built of behaviors and denials) is what we bear, we are in deep trouble.

Giving

- *Malachi 3:8*—"Will a man rob God? Yet you are robbing Me! But you say, 'How have we robbed Thee?' In tithes and offerings."
- *Luke 6:38*—"Give, and it will be given to you; good measure, pressed down, shaken together, running over, they will pour into your lap. For by your standard of measure it will be measured to you in return."
- *2 Corinthians 9:6*—"Now this I say, he who sows sparingly shall also reap sparingly; and he who sows bountifully shall also reap bountifully."

The list of verses used to get people to give in order to please God is long indeed. Give to *get on* God's good side; give to *stay* on His good side; and give in order to *get*. Perhaps it's true that wrong teaching on this subject actually gets people to give by appealing to their greed.

What about giving because you "owe it" to the church? One friend of ours received a letter from the leadership in her church shaming her for not giving to the church even though she attended and received all of the services. The letter went on to say that they had been keeping track for over a year, and they were sure she had received more in services than she had paid for. After all, it said, they were a "full-service church."

They then reminded her that there are hundreds of scripture verses that talk about tithes and offerings. The letter even said that Jesus mentioned giving more than He mentioned the need for *repentance*. They closed by saying that there are "a lot of ministries competing for your contribution dollar. If there is any way we can assist you in channeling some of it to your church, we will be more than happy to do so."

Another couple we learned of recently began attending a new church where, as is customary in many churches, they were asked to fill out a "first-timers" card and put it in the offering plate. In addition to including their name and address, they also checked a box that indicated they wished a pastoral visit.

Not long after, the pastor paid them a visit. After about fifteen minutes of small talk, he asked them if he could see their W–2 forms. Stunned, they asked why; to which he replied, "So we can see what would be the appropriate amount of money you should give based on 10 percent of your income." Feeling very intruded upon, yet keeping her cool, the woman answered, "I'll show you mine if you show me yours." You can guess what his answer was.

What about tithing? The concept only appears infrequently in the New Testament, and then in a very negative light (Matthew 23:23; Luke 18:9–12). Tithing originated in the Old Testament. Actually, there were three separate tithes that totaled about 27.1 percent: 10 percent for the Levites; 10 percent of the rest to support the national festivals; and 10 percent of the rest for the poor. This was non-optional giving. In that day the Israelites had a form of government called a *theocracy,* which means they were under the rule of God and the religious system. These tithes simply amounted to "tax monies" needed to run the country. The 27.1 percent it cost to live in that church-state is similar to the non-optional amount of money we pay to live in our *democracy:* taxes.

How should we view giving? Giving is, and has always been, a *heart* issue. Exodus 25 contains the account of raising the financial resources to construct the sanctuary. God said to Moses, "Tell the sons of Israel to raise a contribution for Me; from every man *whose heart moves him* you shall raise My contribution" (v. 2). After almost 10 chapters of specifications concerning the sanctuary, Moses repeats the condition of the giving. In Exodus 35 he says, "This is the thing which the Lord has commanded, saying, 'Take from among you a contribution to the Lord; *whoever is of a willing heart . . .*' " (vv. 4–5).

In 2 Corinthians 9, Paul says, "Let each one do just as *he has purposed in his heart;* not grudgingly or under compulsion; for *God loves a cheerful giver*" (v. 7). In the next verse, Paul reveals the source from which a heart to give comes: *"And God is able to make all grace abound to you, that always having all sufficiency in everything, you may have an abundance for every good deed."* Do you think that believing that verse would have an impact on giving? We do.

Finally, for those who give in order to get, in Romans 11 Paul asks a rhetorical question: "Or who has first given to [God] that it might be paid back to him again?" (v. 35). The answer: No one. No one has really given to God because all things come from Him. We do reap what we sow in a spiritual sense. There are rewards for good works. These are true statements. But if we sow or work to *earn* a reward, or to put God in a position of owing us, we get nothing. God owes no one anything. And Matthew 6:1–4 says that if you give in order to be noticed or to gain someone's approval, you have your reward already. In other words, you have been "receipted" in full, and your only reward is that someone noticed.

Unity and Peace in the Church

- *Matthew 5:9*—"Blessed are the peacemakers, for they shall be called the sons of God."
- *Philippians 2:2*—"Make my joy complete by being of the same mind, maintaining the same love, united in spirit, intent on one purpose."
- *Ephesians 4:3*—". . . being diligent to preserve the unity of the Spirit in the bond of peace."

Peace and unity are important in the body of Christ. But experiencing true peace and unity does not mean pretending to get along or acting like we agree when we don't. Verses like these have been used to get people to act unified when they are not. The result is a "can't-talk" relationship system in which problems get swept under the carpet and leaders are not held accountable for their actions. Because the people are not really unified at all, dissension and strife grow through gossip and backstabbing.

If you look closely at the Philippians verse you will see the word "maintaining." The Ephesians verse uses the word "preserve." In order to protect peace and unity they have to already exist. It is not possible to preserve or maintain something that is not there. In a spiritually abusive system, people are taught how to counterfeit peace and unity. The irony is that what is actually maintained is a *lack* of peace and unity.

From the field of counseling, we draw in the concept of the person in a dysfunctional family system who keeps or enforces a false peace, a person known as the "peace-keeper." This is the person in a relationship system who gets in the middle of everyone else's relationships and tries to help them ignore their problems with one another. They usually take responsibility for everyone getting along. Actually, "peace-keeper" is not an accurate description of this person, because to keep peace there has to be peace to keep. They are more of a "truce-maker." A truce is an agreement to cease fighting between people who are still at odds and who have yet to work out their differences. What the truce-maker wants to avoid, again, is any appearance that there is conflict in the system, or, in a spiritual system, that the leaders have anything wrong with them that might cause others to be in conflict with them. Conflict would be a sign of something wrong, and, according to the unspoken rules, there cannot be anything wrong.

A true peacemaker, as noted in Matthew 5, is someone who goes where there is no peace and makes peace. It is *not* someone who covers over disagreement with a cloak of false peace. It is not someone who gets people who are in total disagreement to act as if they are on the same side. For real peace to happen, not just a cease-fire, there has to be a change of heart. Where does that come from?

In James 3, the apostle writes:

> But if you have bitter jealousy and selfish ambition *in your heart*, do not be arrogant and so lie against the truth. This wisdom is not that which comes down from above, but is earthly, natural, demonic. For *where jealousy and selfish ambition exist, there is disorder* and every evil thing. But the wisdom from above is *first pure, then peaceable*, gentle, reasonable, full of mercy and good fruits, unwavering, without hypocrisy. And the seed whose fruit is righteousness is sown in peace by those who make peace. (vv. 14–18)

Notice, first, that James is reminding us that jealousy and strife are issues of the *heart*. Notice also that where these things are present, there is disorder. In other words, the presence of disorder simply signals a problem in the heart. That is why getting people to smooth things over doesn't help and will only eventually make things worse. Notice, too, that wisdom is first of all *pure*; peace comes after purity. The word "pure" means undefiled, genuine, true. Wisdom brings peace through *truth*, not truce.

Paul says in Ephesians 5, "And do not participate in the unfruitful deeds of darkness, but instead even expose them. . . . But all things become visible when they are exposed by the light, for everything that becomes visible is light" (vv. 11, 13). Accountability, change of heart, and even peace are possible in the light of the truth. Darkness is where wrongdoing and confusion operate. James calls false peace and hypocrisy *demonic*.

Church Discipline

- *Matthew 18:15–17*—"And if your brother sins, go and reprove him in private; if he listens to you, you have won your brother. But if he does not listen to you, take one or two more with you, so that by the mouth of two or three witnesses every fact may be confirmed. And if he refuses to listen to them, tell it to the church; and if he refuses to listen even to the church, let him be to you as a Gentile and a tax-gatherer."
- *1 Corinthians 5:5*—"I have decided to deliver such a one to Satan for the destruction of his flesh, that his spirit may be saved in the day of the Lord Jesus."

These verses are "church discipline" verses. Church discipline is a very crucial, often misunderstood and sometimes abusive issue among Christians. It is crucial in two contexts: reconciliation among fellow Christians; and protecting people from danger in the body of Christ.

In a spiritually abusive system, these verses become weapons in the hands of performance-based people to get people to act differently, or to get rid of them if they do not.

Context, once again, is very helpful in understanding the heart of these two passages. In Matthew 18, the verses immediately preceding describe a sheep that has gone astray. So the shepherd leaves the rest of his sheep to go look for the one that has wandered off. In 1 Corinthians 5, the issue is a person who is in an incestuous relationship with his father's wife, perhaps a step-mother. The shocking news is out, since it has been commonly reported (v. 1), and the problem is having a negative effect on the entire church (v. 6).

The brother that has sinned against you is like the sheep who wandered off. Consequently, "*go* and reprove him." In other words, *go get him* and bring him back. If he doesn't listen, get some others and go again. If he still does not listen, tell the church. "Church" does not mean the group of people that meet together under the same roof a couple of times a week; it is the group of people who have a genuine spiritual connection with the wandering person. If he still does not listen, let him go. (We will talk more in the next chapter about the phrase "let him be to you as a Gentile and a tax-gatherer.")

It's a different story in 1 Corinthians. This is not a person who has wandered off. This man is sinning right in the middle of the body and everyone knows it. His sin is affecting the whole body. Why? Because in relationship systems like families and churches, what one member does affects all of the members. Now it's easy to see how someone who is a sexual perpetrator has a negative effect on his or her victims. But what about an affair, as in this case? Since everyone in the church knew about it, they were affected because they had the burden of keeping this knowledge hidden. It takes just as much energy to *not* deal with problems as to deal with them. Actually it takes more energy—because in not dealing with problems, you get to keep the problem plus you have to work hard to cover it up.

In this case, Paul is very stern. He is upset that the Corinthians had not felt the weight of the situation "in order that the one who had done this deed might be removed from your midst." In verses 9–10 he reminds them that by his instruction "not to associate with immoral people; I did not at all mean with the immoral people of this world . . . for then you would have to go out of the world." Paul was not paranoid about what went on outside, but concerned about what went on inside. His warning concerned "any so-called brother, if he should be an immoral person."

This is difficult to enforce in some churches, however, because those who need to be disciplined are in charge.

Conclusion

The greatest value of this chapter is not in attempting to untangle every example of scriptural abuse; this would be impossible. Our hope is that you have gained clarity on some issues.

But more than that, our desire is for you to have gained some perspective on how to approach Scripture, how to let Scripture approach you, and how to hold others accountable for "rightly dividing" Scripture, as well.

As you have seen, the Word of God *is* like a powerful sword. It can be used as an instrument of grace by bringing reminders of God's love. It can bring order to our lives. In the wrong hands, or wrongfully used, it can be used to put weights on people and shame them into performing someone's agenda in the name of God.

In the next chapter, we'll look at how God's Word has been misused specifically in the lives of hurt, victimized people in such a way as to abuse them all over again.

"You shall know the truth and the truth shall set you free." For those who have been wounded emotionally, physically and spiritually, the beginning of their freedom comes in admitting the truth of their struggles and asking for help. Revictimization occurs when the truth is suppressed in the name of spirituality. And it is even more devastating when the code of silence is enforced with God's own Word, the very source of truth.

8

Revictimizing Victims

God breathed His Word to give us life, to equip us to live, and to guide us through life.

As Paul says in 2 Timothy 3, "All Scripture is inspired by God and profitable for teaching, for reproof, for correction, for training in righteousness; that the man [in Greek, *person*] of God may be adequate, equipped for every good work" (vv. 16–17). Psalm 119 amounts to a 176-verse tribute to God's Word. In verse 105 the Psalmist says, "Thy word is a lamp to my feet, and a light to my path."

Sometimes, however, because of how God's Word has been applied, it has not been a help but a hindrance. Instead of a lamp and a light leading people in the path of truth, it has been employed as a tool to keep in the dark those secrets that destroy families and churches. Instead of being "revived by His precepts" (Psalm 119:93), some victims of various kinds of abuse have been further abused and betrayed as the Word has been misused to minimize their pain and excuse their perpetrators. For some, healing has been short-circuited: Jesus' precept, "the truth will set you free," has been replaced by man's precepts, "to be nice is better than to be honest" and "keep the (false) peace at all costs."

This chapter will show a few of the ways wounded people have experienced God's Word in an unhelpful, even revictimizing way. Let's look at them.

Never Resist

- *Matthew 5:39*—"But I say to you, do not resist him who is evil; but whoever slaps you on your right cheek, turn to him the other also."

Is Jesus serious? Yes, He is—more serious than most of us realize. But is Jesus, whose Father in the Old Testament had His people annihilate armies and wipe out entire countries for being evil, really telling people not to fight against evil? Or worse yet, is He really suggesting that we should leave ourselves in harm's way? This, in fact, *is* the advice that many already victimized people receive in abusive systems.

This verse is often used to encourage abuse victims to stay in bad situations and continue being abused. This verse is often wrongly quoted to people who have been humiliated or given bad counsel by Christian leaders.

There are several things to notice about the context in which this passage falls. First, it is found in a chapter that begins with, "Blessed are the poor in spirit, for theirs is the kingdom of heaven," and ends with, "Therefore you are to be perfect, as your heavenly Father is perfect." Second, it falls in a particular section that begins with, "For I say to you, that unless your righteousness surpasses that of the scribes and Pharisees, you shall not enter the kingdom of heaven." Third, it is preceded by the verse, "You have heard it said, 'An eye for an eye, and a tooth for a tooth.' "

To understand this passage, we must raise some questions. Does being "poor in spirit" result in getting a person into heaven, or is it the person who achieves "righteousness that surpasses that of the scribes and Pharisees"? Which is it? And how can we ever hope to be perfect as our heavenly Father is perfect? Is Jesus giving abuse victims a prescription for how they should *live*, or is He raising the issue of how a person *enters the kingdom*?

How these issues are understood has great impact, both eternally and on how we live in the meantime. First, He is teaching the disciples about issues that will concern the multitude—lepers, prostitutes, tax-gatherers, and Pharisees. He is not telling wounded people that it is somehow spiritually virtuous to allow themselves to be wounded again. Yet religious helpers counseled many people who have been propelled back into abusive relationships through the use of this verse, even though the context clearly indicates that the issue is that of righteousness and how a person enters the kingdom.

When faced with the prospect of having righteousness that surpasses that of the Pharisees, the wrong response is to try hard. The correct response is to look at your lack of righteousness and your own inability to generate it and say, "I can't do that." Now we have a broken person, poor in spirit. The kingdom belongs to broken people.

Likewise, when faced with the prospect of trying to be perfect like God, the wrong response is to try hard. The right response is to fall on our face in the presence of God's perfect grace and say, "I can't do it. I need a gift." Hebrews 7:19 says, "[for the Law made nothing perfect], and on the other hand there is a bringing in of a better hope, through which we draw near to God." And now look at Hebrews 10:14: "For by one offering He has perfected for all time those who are sanctified."

"An eye for an eye" (Matthew 5:38) was the form of justice instituted in the Old Testament to protect victims from people who were more powerful or affluent. But the heart of the rule was not vengeance ("Make sure you get an eye for an eye!"), it was, "Make sure you *only* get an eye for an eye."

At the time of Jesus, the Pharisees (the religiously powerful and affluent) were making sure they got an eye for an eye. After all, those are the rules. By reminding them of the rule, Jesus has already confronted their heart as it is revealed by their response to human offenses: *The legalist will always want to see another punished, or made to perform as a compensation for weakness or sin.*

Then Jesus goes on to say something that would have been heard very differently, depending on the listener. "Let yourself be victimized again." To the poor, powerless victims of the system, it probably sounded like business as usual. After all, what could they do to prevent it anyway? To a Pharisee, however, it would have sounded ludicrous. This wasn't playing by the rules. What did Jesus mean? To find out what He meant, they would have to follow after Him, listen and observe as He *lived out* the answer. And so must we.

The Greek language indicates that the kind of slap to which Jesus was referring was a backhand slap. This was not merely an act of violence, it was an act of disdain. For the one slapped, it was extremely humiliating. Picture the powerful, self-righteous Pharisees, adorned in religious splendor, who "love the place of honor . . . and respectful greetings in the market places." How would a person whose heart was like this respond to Jesus' command? If the response Jesus wanted was one of compliance, the result would be a slapped-up Pharisee, who thought he was even more righteous than before.

But an average Pharisee, who gets his sense of identity, value, and meaning from what people think, could never take a backhand slap. The normal person would respond, "I could never do that—I must be a spiritual failure." At this point Jesus had a "poor in spirit" person. And "blessed are the poor in spirit, for theirs is the Kingdom of Heaven." Jesus offered a gift to spiritual failures.

Wives, Submit—Even if it Kills You

We have counseled far too many Christian women who were being brutalized, emotionally crushed, even bloodied *by Christian hus-*

bands. And we have listened, appalled, to the "counsel" given by pastors and other spiritual leaders to these wounded daughters of God all too often: "Wives, submit to your husbands . . ." This mishandling of Scripture is, sadly, widespread, and used to press abused women into staying in destructive situations. We offer one of many case histories.

Charlotte was being battered by her husband. She would spend her days planning what to do and not do so she would not get beat up when he got home from work. As he came in the door she would enact all the things she planned. But inevitably Charlotte would do something "wrong" (a phrase, an action, a look on her face) and the abuse would start. At first it was verbal abuse. He would loom over her, calling her names and using hideous profanity. It would escalate to shoving. Then he would hit her with his open hand, but being careful to do so only in places on her body where clothes would conceal the bruises. This happened on a regular basis over a period of six years.

In addition, during most of the marriage Charlotte's husband had been involved in numerous affairs with single and married women, including teenagers and friends of his wife. At the same time he was active in the church.

One night the abuse was so bad, Charlotte's nine-year-old son got out of bed and ran to the front door. With his mom screaming for him to go and his dad screaming for him to stop, he ran to a neighbor's house and called the police. They answered the call, arrested the husband, and the abuse was over—temporarily.

Charlotte went to the leaders in her church. She told them about the length and degree of abuse. She told them about the incident with her son. They listened supportively, for a while. With tear-filled eyes she was finally able to say, "I am afraid for my life. I don't think I can stay with my husband anymore."

Their response was *not* what she needed to hear: "If you leave your husband, you will be out of the will of God. You must stay." They also said that her son had been disobedient and should have listened to his father, God's covering over him.

There was no support. No help. And their statement added despair to despair. Her heartache was multiplied as these men she trusted subjected her to an hour-long Bible verse session, "proving" their point.

The travesty of how abused women are silenced and made to

remain in abusive situations through the use of God's Word is as widespread as it is appalling. Charlotte's case, though one woman's story, will sound like the stories of many victims of scriptural abuse. What did Charlotte hear in that hour-long Bible session?

First, she was told that if she left her husband, she would be depriving her children of the "heritage" of observing a "godly response to suffering." They told her, "Children learn more by example than by talk." Then they referred her to 1 Peter 2:13–15:

> Submit yourselves for the Lord's sake to every authority instituted among men: whether to the king, as the supreme authority, or to governors, who are sent by him to punish those who do wrong . . . for it is God's will that by doing good you should silence the ignorant talk of foolish men. (NIV)

First of all, it's important to note that this passage is addressed to slaves, not wives. The fact that it was quoted to Charlotte says more, perhaps, about the view these men have about wives. In fact, in chapter 3 verse 7 of the same epistle, Peter urges husbands to live with wives in an understanding way, to grant them honor, and to treat them as fellow-heirs of God's grace. This behavior on the part of husbands would run exactly contrary to the ancient view (and all too prevalent present view) of women as inferior beings. His reference to women as weaker vessels refers to their physical vulnerability—a quality to be understood, not exploited. In fact, Peter insinuates that God doesn't hear the prayers of husbands who act contrary to this instruction.

In 1 Peter 3:1–2, the apostle instructs wives to submit to husbands who are disobedient to the Word, in order that they may be won to God. This directly follows a passage (in chapter 2) that talks about persevering when you are mistreated because you have done right. The larger context begins with 1 Peter 2:13, with the instruction to submit to human institutions that are sent by God "for the punishment of evildoers and the praise of those who do right."

Now we must ask: Who is the evildoer in an abusive marriage— the husband who is abusive, or the wife who exposes a crime?

It is *not* "evil" for the wife to expose a crime. It would be wrong to keep quiet and stay, or leave the relationship and say nothing. The bigger question that needs to be asked is this: Is Peter telling Christians in general, and then slaves and wives in particular, to do right *by* submitting, or is he telling them to do right *and* submit? Because of the larger context, we have come to the conclusion that Peter is telling Christians to do right *and* submit. How would an abused Christian do right and submit at the same time? We believe it would be to stay in the relationship with the person—if necessary from a safe, protected distance—and at the same time to hold the accuser accountable to the laws of the land for the abuse. This represents, in our opinion, the *most* caring, submissive response for everyone involved.

One of the most severe abuses of these particular passages was told to me by a woman who had an interaction with her pastor. She told him about the fact that she had recently been strangled to unconsciousness by her husband and felt she needed to escape to safety. His response? "Stay with him and if he kills you, God will use that to draw him to himself." Another person (Jesus) had already died to get the husband's attention, but not even that had worked.

Friends in Christ, this is sad, sick counsel.

This is the "heritage" that is being left to the children in families where abusers are not held accountable: Eighty-five percent of men who batter their wives, and thirty percent of their victims, grew up in violent homes.[1] Abusers are made, not born.[2] So you see, Charlotte's leaders did make a statement that was true. Children do learn more from example than from words. In a family where violence is observed by the children but not addressed in a healthy way, little boys and girls learn perverted views of how men and women are to relate to each other. This heritage is right from the pit of hell.

Just Forgive

- *Matthew 18:21–22*—"Then Peter came and said to Him, 'Lord, how often shall my brother sin against me and I forgive him? Up to seven times?' Jesus said to him, 'I do not say to you, up to seven times, but up to seventy times seven.' "

This is another verse that can be terribly abusive if taken out of context and used against Christians for the wrong reasons. It is so frequently misused that we feel it's necessary to take some time to explore the true meaning.

Misapplications of this vary, including: "Don't notice the abuse," "What's wrong with you that you can't forgive?" and "You have an unforgiving spirit, or a root of bitterness." It has also been used to get people to *act* as if they forgive an offender before they really do. When

---

[1]Strauss, Gelles, and Steinmetz, *Behind Closed Doors: Violence in the American Family* (New York: Anchor Books, 1980).

[2]Kay Marshall Strom, *In the Name of Submission* (Portland, Oregon: Multnomah Press, 1986).

this happens they continue to struggle with forgiving them over and over again, and are indicted because they haven't been able to let the matter drop. But the matter cannot be dropped because wrong was never addressed.

Once again, the context is very helpful. This passage falls within a chapter that begins with the disciples' question, "Who then is the greatest in the kingdom of heaven?" The chapter ends with a story of an unforgiving servant and a king who, moved with anger against this person, "handed him over to the torturers until he should repay all that was owed him." The final verse in the chapter contains Jesus' warning, "So shall My heavenly Father also do to you, if each of you does not forgive his brother *from your heart*."

Again, the emphasis is on integrity, purity of heart rather than covering up.

We have already discussed Matthew 18:15–17 in the previous chapter. We want to say more at this time about Jesus' statement in verse 17, "Let [a willing sinner] be to you as a Gentile and a tax-gatherer."

First, to a Jew, a Gentile was a person to stay away from, because being with them could lead to ritual defilement. Second, tax-gatherers in a way were even worse. A tax-gatherer was a Jewish person who collected taxes for the Romans—someone who was supposed to be on your side but who was working for the enemy. Again, stay away.

Jesus did not say *"make* him be . . ." He said *"let* him be." Your choice to stay away from this person does not cause him to be anything. His own hurtful actions and refusal to repent make him the unsafe person that he is. You are simply acknowledging the reality of the situation.

Even so, Jesus proposed that there be three confrontations before you give up on an offender. That is because three times was Jewish tradition: After three times you could give up on the person knowing that you had done your part. It is in that light that we need to understand Peter's question, "Up to seven times?" It is as if he is thinking, "If three is good, seven is even better." Peter seems to be searching for the formula for how to be the greatest, which is the question that began the chapter. In this context, Peter appears to be trying to discover how to achieve righteousness based on how forgiving you are.

Jesus gives His answer, "Seventy times seven." Four hundred and ninety times! Then is that the magic number? Can we stop at 490? Are we righteous after that? What if Peter's question had been, "How many times should I forgive my brother—490 times?" We believe Jesus would have said, "No, seventy times seventy times seven." He wasn't trying to tell people a right number when it comes to forgiving. He was pushing the standard out past the range of human performance. Upon hearing Jesus' answer, our response should not be to try hard to forgive someone more times. Our response should be, "Where does that kind of forgiveness come from? No matter how hard I try I can't do that." Our response should be, "If that's the case, I give up. I'm poor in spirit."

Do you remember Jesus' warning? He who cannot forgive from *the heart* will find himself handed over to the torturers. Jesus is telling us many things with this story; first, that one "from-the-heart" forgiveness is better than 490 "forgivenesses" that come from trying hard or pretending. In other words, forgiveness is so important that it must be *real*. Second, he is showing where true forgiveness comes from. It doesn't come from self-effort, designed to meet some standard. It comes from realizing our desperate situation and that our only hope is in God's mercy, and then letting it flow into our hearts.

That was the man's problem in the parable of the debtor who owed the king the great sum of money. When asked to pay a debt he couldn't, his response was not one of brokenness—he didn't ask for mercy. He said, "Give me some time and I will pay." No wonder he was unforgiving toward his fellow slave who owed him a little. The first man never accepted the great forgiveness available to him.

Finally, this teaching follows Jesus' charge to let an unrepentant offender "be as a tax-gatherer." I think this means that it is possible both to forgive someone and still stay away from them. Forgiving someone means you release them from debt. It does not necessarily mean you are going to trust them, or have a close relationship with them again. As Luke 17:3 says, "Be on your guard! If your brother sins, rebuke him; and *if he repents* forgive him." Notice that in this passage, our forgiveness of another is based on their repentance.

Conditional forgiveness? Does God forgive those who don't repent? Does God hold us accountable to do something He himself is unwilling to do? We only know that we are to forgive. But "from the heart" forgiveness results from the process of realizing our own need for forgiveness and letting in God's mercy, not from covering up hurt, or trying hard to forgive enough times.

Never Appeal to Secular Authorities

- *1 Corinthians 6:1-2*—"Does any one of you, when he has a case against his neighbor, dare to go to law before the unrighteous, and not before the saints? Or do you not know that the saints will judge the world? And if the world is judged by you, are you not competent to constitute the smallest law courts?"

A woman who was filing criminal charges against a former pastor for sexually exploiting her during their counseling relationship was told, "It's judgmental and unchristian for you to take him to court. It's against 1 Corinthians 6!" She was being told to shut up, though little or nothing was being done to rectify the problem. The results of the abuse of this Scripture are that offenders are not held accountable for their behavior, and they are even allowed to continue in their sin.

What this passage is referring to is a *civil suit*. In a civil case, one party is the plaintiff (going to law with a case against his neighbor) and one is the defendant. More than likely, Paul is referring to a fight between Christians over a cow, a piece of property, or a sum of money. He affirms the fact that the ability to decide such matters lies within the body of Christ. Unfortunately, in some places the saints are part of the cover-up.

If the passage was referring to a criminal case, then Paul's Romans 13 instructions concerning governing authorities are meaningless. Indeed, Romans 13 is the passage that refers to God's provision for dealing with criminal activities. In a criminal case the state is the plaintiff. The governing authorities are God's sword, used to avenge wrongdoing.

In the case of the sexually assaulted woman, what the pastor did was illegal. But for all her humiliation, she was further abused— accused during the case by scores of people in the church of trying to seduce the pastor. But even if she did try to seduce him, while that would have been immoral, what he did was illegal. Her behavior would not justify his. There is no legal reason for a pastor to become sexually involved with a counselee. *Someone* is supposed to be the healthy person: Shouldn't it be the spiritual helper?

This was not an instance of someone going to court against a neighbor. It was a case of the governing authorities going to court against someone for breaking the laws of the land. The woman was a witness for the state because she was the victim of the crime. When a pastor or counselor becomes sexually involved with a counselee, it is a crime. When a husband batters his wife, it is a crime. When a parent abuses or neglects a child, it is a crime. Reporting a crime does not go against 1 Corinthians 6. Being a Christian does not exempt someone from being held legally accountable for their behaviors.

Never Deal with the Past

- *Philippians 3:13–14*—"... forgetting what lies behind and reaching forward to what lies ahead, I press on toward the goal for the prize of the upward call of God in Christ Jesus."

Many we have counseled have had this verse used to prod them into silence about the painful, unresolved issues of the past.

One man who began to talk about the abuse in his family started getting placards containing this and other verses through the mail. He would also find them on his dresser, dashboard and refrigerator.

A victim who goes along with this abusive application of this passage will freeze up their pain and, more than likely, find themselves in a state of depression or some other more severe form of emotional distress later on.

What Paul is really referring to in this passage is all of his *religious performance* from which he used to draw his sense of spiritual life and acceptance. In verses 1–3 of this chapter, he reminds us to rejoice in the Lord, not in our religious behavior. In verses 4-6, he makes a list of all the things he did in the name of God, attempting to find spiritual life and meaning. In verses 7–11, he says that he left his list behind and considers it trash "for the sake of the surpassing value of knowing Christ." And in verses 12–16, he describes the process of living in the spiritual presence of Jesus, so as to be transformed, rather than performing according to some list. He is focused upon Jesus, and leaves behind his own religious behavior as the means of getting accepted by God.

Conclusion: God Is *For* Those Who Hurt

Matthew 12:15–21 contains a wonderful, encouraging description of Jesus' stance toward those who are broken and wounded. He healed all who were brought to him (v. 15), and He brought justice to the Gentiles (v. 18). But look at verse 20: "A battered reed he will not break off, and a smoldering wick He will not put out."

Are you feeling like a battered reed? God is *for* you, to make you straight and strong once again. Are you a smoldering wick? His Spirit is yours, to fan your broken heart to a passionate flame toward Him and others. God will not throw us out if we are broken.

God does not have a problem with our pain, or with our process of coming to spiritual health. In 2 Corinthians 7, Paul himself admits to exhaustion, fear and depression. But he also rejoices in "God, who comforts the depressed" (v. 7).

Part II

Abusive Leaders and Why They Are Trapped

Introduction

Jesus and Leaders

In Part I, we have given an overview of a spiritually abusive system (whether it be a family, ministry, or church). This included its identifying characteristics; what makes it attractive to spiritually hungry people; its main component, which is leadership that postures spiritual power rather than demonstrating real spiritual authority; and how the abusive system continues to reabuse victims.

In Part II, the focus is on the central power figures in the abusive system: the leaders. Without a strong, central figure or figures who claim to have authoritative knowledge of God, an abusive system cannot attract followers who are hungering for the Life of God. Nor can it, conversely, keep them trapped. We will present the problem these leaders create in as serious a light as we believe it to be.

We must preface this section by acknowledging that we believe many legalistic, controlling, and ultimately abusive leaders may simply have lost sight of, or never experienced, the life of grace in Christ. Many, through no fault of their own, have been taught legalism or formula Christianity. Others, perhaps through ministry burnout, have simply forgotten the simple, wonder-filled, joyous relationship each one of us can experience with God because of Jesus Christ. Still others have innocently come under one of the various "Authority" movements that periodically sweep through the church—usually variations on the same heresy, that "vision" or "guidance" must come only through a spiritual "head" (pastor, elder, group leader, husband, etc.), ultimately denying an individual's ability to hear from God.

That is to say, we enter this section acknowledging the possibility of innocence on the part of any spiritual leaders who may see themselves in what we portray. It's our hope that any leader who has left grace behind in order to follow another revelation will see his error and return to his "first love" (Revelation 2:4–5). We hope that others may realize their own sinful need to be viewed as powerful or beyond correction, and that these leaders will recognize the transgression of laying heavy weights of spiritual performance upon God's children.

To do so, we will focus on Jesus' confrontations with the spiritual leaders of His day. We believe everyone can benefit from combing through this collision of *grace* versus *spiritual performance.*

Most important, we offer an invitation from the Father of Love: *Today, turn from your works and drop your heavy weights; follow Me to real freedom and rest.*

Have you ever heard one kid say to another, "Who died and made you king?" This question usually arises when one person has taken charge of the group, usually by virtue of being older, bigger, stronger or louder. It also betrays frustration on the part of his "subjects."

This is exactly the dynamic Jesus faced in the religious system of His day. And it is the first tip-off to spiritual leadership that is false.

9

"Because I'm the Pastor, That's Why!"

Several months ago, I (David speaking) met with a young couple who were seeking advice concerning a very important issue. Their problem had no easy answer, but I did my best to give them some direction. Their response to everything I said was instantly, overwhelmingly positive. Rather than feeling exceptionally smart or spiritual, I actually felt uncomfortable. My advice wasn't *that* good! I began to get the sense that no matter what I said they would agree, and they would probably do whatever I said, as well.

Please understand my hesitance: This couple was bright, intelligent, and highly successful in their careers. So what was wrong with this picture? I realized that when it came to spiritual issues, they somehow put their minds on "hold." I realized that the total responsibility to discern and decide had been turned over to the pastor—in this case, me.

Lights began to go on as I began to ask about this couple's spiritual history. It was one of blatant spiritual abuse under a pastor whose "words are from God." To question or disobey him meant to question and disobey God. "Touch not the Lord's anointed" was the motto most repeated if anyone disagreed with him. Anyone who suggested that something was wrong quickly became "the problem."

As if to demonstrate the far-ranging power of such a system, the residue of its mindset clung to these folks, even though they had made their escape from it some time ago. They were willing to blindly submit to an authority figure (me) and accept my words solely on the basis of my position. People with savvy in every other area of their lives turned to mush when it came time to discern spiritual things. That responsibility was handed over to me. Why? Because I'm the pastor, that's why.

False Authority

"Because I'm the pastor, that's why!" The words come hard and fast, their meaning penetrates: "How dare you doubt me!" "Are you questioning my authority?" "Don't be a troublemaker." "Keep the peace." "Submit to your elder."

Scripture verses quickly come to mind in seeming support of a blind sort of obedience and submission. Hebrews 13:17: "Obey your leaders, and submit to them; for they keep watch over your souls, as those who will give an account." Romans 13:1–2: "Let every person be in subjection to the governing authorities. For there is no authority except from God, and those which exist are established by God. Therefore he who resists authority has opposed the ordinance of God; and they who have opposed will receive condemnation upon themselves."

With these Scriptures echoing, we tell ourselves, *I believe the Bible. I want to be obedient. He's the pastor, the shepherd, God's servant, His mouthpiece. He really must know more than me. I really must be out of line. I must be seeing this wrong. Who am I to question? I guess I had just better go along. Why? Because he's the pastor, that's why.*

This type of thinking is a symptom of living under leadership that legislates and demands obedience to their authority. It rests upon *a false basis of authority.*

Jesus confronted false spiritual authority in His day:

> Then Jesus spoke to the multitudes and to His disciples, saying, 'The scribes and the Pharisees have seated themselves in the chair of Moses." (Matthew. 23:1)

The "chair of Moses" referred to by Jesus is, of course, not a literal chair. Rather it speaks of a "seat of authority." For instance, the "chair" of the philosophy department in a college is not a literal chair, but speaks of an earned place or position of authority in that department. The Greek word for "chair" is *cathedra.* The Latin has taken that word and made it a phrase, *ex-cathedra,* which means "to speak out of a place of authority." If I speak *ex-cathedra,* using that to place myself in a position over you, what I say to you is binding. The reason it is binding is because I speak *ex-cathedra.* I speak from the seat of authority.

Jesus' confrontation is twofold. First, He pointed out that "they seated themselves" in Moses' position—a position given only by God. These men had *taken* authority for themselves, it had not been *given* to them. Second, the sole basis on which they had grasped this authority was because of their position or rank as scribes and Pharisees. In other words, their authority was not founded on the fact that they were wise, discerning and true. It was based solely in the fact that they were in charge.

Think about this for a moment. What a convenient system! This is a system that will let you be in control, even if you are: a Pharisee whose outward holiness hides an empty heart; a scribe who is an expert at little more than rote religious performance; a pastor who doesn't want to look inside; an elder who doesn't want others to know there are serious problems in your own family.

A Maddening Attitude

Using rank, position, status, or title as a sole basis of spiritual authority reminds us of the maddening attitude concerning the role of women in the church, a residue, we believe, of the old Hebrew system of governing.

In Israel, the criteria for leadership and authority was based on three things. The first criterion was age: You had to be old. Second, gender: You had to be male. And third, race: You had to be Hebrew. Obviously, it was a great system for old Hebrew males. In that system, you did not have to be right, wise, gentle, discerning, Spirit-directed, or godly. If you were a young Gentile woman, it wouldn't matter if you were wise, gentle, discerning, or Spirit-directed. You didn't have authority because you didn't fit the external criteria.

But consider Acts 2. The Holy Spirit came and blew that system to pieces when the prophesy of Joel was fulfilled at Pentecost: "I will pour forth of My spirit upon *all mankind*; and your sons and your *daughters* shall prophesy, and your *young men* shall see visions, and your old men shall dream dreams. Even upon My *bondslaves, both men and women*, I will in those days pour forth of My Spirit" (vv. 17–18).

In the new covenant, then, we see that Jesus established a new basis of authority. It was no longer age, gender, or race. It is now based on the evidence of the Holy Spirit within you. Attributes like maturity, wisdom, genuine holiness, and real knowledge are required in order to evidence Jesus' brand of authority. "Because I said so" does not work anymore. "Because I'm the pastor" does not cut it. So if my basis for authority is *solely* that I hold an office, I have a false basis of authority.

Let's get a biblical perspective on true spiritual authority considering some examples of those who demonstrated it.

The first is *Moses*. Moses clearly demonstrated the authority of one who had come to know God through a personal relationship. In fact, it was his very authority that the scribes and Pharisees were presuming for themselves. Moses was to them *the* authority. But even his authority wasn't his. Just because Moses made a pronouncement didn't mean it was automatically authoritative. His authority came from the fact that he truthfully and clearly told the people *exactly what God told him*. If God had given him something to say and Moses had turned it around, somehow making it different, he would not have had authority. The only legitimate authority that Moses had was when he spoke exactly what God told him to say.

What does this mean? It means that *the authority* was in the truth, not in Moses. It wasn't because Moses was Moses, someone higher, better, more powerful than others; it was because he spoke the truth. Because Moses was a servant who did what God told him to do no matter what the cost, he walked in what is the only appropriate basis of spiritual authority.

From Moses, we must draw this conclusion: Though people may honor us with a position of leadership, we do not have authority in God's eyes simply because we are named the pastor, the elder, or the chairman. *We are going to have to speak the truth to have authority.* We are going to have to be sensitive to the Spirit to have authority. We are going to have to be wise, and seek to know and say what God says clearly and accurately.

Is it possible for any one person to have such a strong record of leading and governing in God's authority? Yes, but this is rare. Is it possible that a small group of elders can have such a record on behalf of a whole group of people? Yes, but again this is rare. The point here is that it is also possible that God speaks, in some way, by His Spirit, through every man and woman in a given body, contributing various facets of God's will, so that the leaders can gain an even clearer picture of what God wants to accomplish. In fact, this is what Acts 2 indicates.

The next example is *Timothy*. Timothy was the pastor of the church in Ephesus, a large church previously led by Paul. Timothy was having difficulty establishing authority in his ministry. Following the apostle

Paul in the pastorate would be a formidable task for anyone, but for Timothy it was particularly troublesome. Not having some of the instinctive, aggressive leadership qualities that Paul had, Timothy was getting run over by strong, negative influences in the church. The epistles of First and Second Timothy are Paul's letters of instruction to Timothy on how to deal with the problem.

At no time did Paul suggest that Timothy puff out his chest and announce boldly, *"I am the pastor!"* No, he said things like this: "Be diligent to present yourself approved to God, as a workman who does not need to be ashamed, handling accurately the word of truth" (2 Timothy 2:15). It is as if Paul took Timothy aside and said, "Son, authority will come when you rightly divide the word of truth. It won't come because you're loud. It won't come because you throw your ecclesiastical weight around. If you want authority, figure out what God has been saying through His Word, tell the people what the Word says, and your authority will be founded upon that."

In 2 Timothy 3:14–17, Paul said:

> You [Timothy], however, continue in the things you have learned and become convinced of, knowing from whom you have learned them; and that from childhood you have known the sacred writings which are able to give you the wisdom that leads to salvation through faith which is in Christ Jesus. All Scripture is inspired by God and profitable for teaching, for reproof, for correction, for training in righteousness; that the man of God may be adequate, equipped for every good work.

Or in simpler words, "If you want to know what to say, go to the Scripture. You'll sound inspired, like you know what you're talking about. Figure out what God says. Timothy, that is your authority base. Give people the Word. Tell people the truth."

Is it possible for one person, or one group of leaders, to comprehend all that's in God's Word? Not likely. God's living Word is demonstrated through all who are seeking Him, regardless of "rank." In some areas of life, many areas perhaps, those in the pews will have more real authority from having tested and lived out God's Word in situations God will never choose to lead the pastor through. If *He* is the Shepherd of the flock, then I as a pastor must listen to what He is saying through the flock, remembering that I too am a follower of Him.

Paul is a third example. While we rightly accept everything Paul has said in the epistles as authoritative, Paul himself warned that just because he says something does not make it true. In Galatians 1:8 he said, "Even though we, or an angel from heaven, should preach to you a gospel contrary to that which we have preached to you, let him be accursed." It's as if Paul is saying, "Listen Galatians, if I start twisting this gospel, don't listen to me. You see, the authority isn't in me. As long as I speak the truth, I will have authority. Authority is not automatically part of a person. The authority is in the truth."

The final example is *Jesus*. When people heard Jesus teach, one of their common responses was amazement. They marveled because they had never experienced such authoritative teaching. It was different than the teaching of the scribes and Pharisees. What they noticed was the authority.

Authenticity

These are four great portraits to relate to the texts we noted earlier. Men like Moses, Timothy, Paul and Jesus could *authenticate* with the fabric of their very lives that their authority was from God. It is in this context that we should view passages like Romans 13:1–2. That is, if someone rebels against living, demonstrated, authentic authority that obviously results from a life submitted to God, then he or she is opposing the governance of God. It does not mean that a leader can take the attitude, "I said it, and I'm the authority so it must be right. And even if it's wrong you should submit to it, because submitting to me is the same as submitting to God." We submit to authority when it demonstrates authenticity.

Even today we have leaders who are like the scribes and Pharisees saying, "I have authority because I am sitting in the chair of authority. I speak *ex-cathedra* to you, binding you to accept and obey all of my words." Because scribes and Pharisees have no real authority, they have to assert their position. They forget or ignore the model Jesus provided when He simply came and spoke the truth. They forget that the basis of His authority was clearly not an office, role, or position, because He had none of these things.

Whenever or wherever we see a system or a person posturing or *assuming* a position of authority based solely on role, office, or position, we are dealing with a false basis of authority. If a person's spiritual authority rests on the sole fact that "I am the pastor," there is a good chance they have taken that posture because they have no *real* authority.

Off to See the Wizard

Many will easily recall the story of "The Wizard of Oz." Curiously, we can gain some insights about spiritual authority from this popular tale. Dorothy, the Scarecrow, the Tin Man and the Cowardly Lion go to the Wizard because they believe he has the power to give them what they need. Dorothy needs to go home; the Scarecrow needs a brain; the Tin Man needs a heart; and the Lion needs courage. The Wizard sends them out on a quest to get the broomstick of the Wicked Witch of the West. If they bring back the broomstick, he will give them what they need. They accomplish their mission by melting the witch and getting the broomstick, then return to the Wizard's place to ask him to deliver on his promise. But, in fact, he is not expecting their return, and is quite put out at being held accountable to keep his promise.

Our heroes enter the huge chamber where the Wizard of Oz conducts his business. They are met face to face by the Wizard himself, a big, scary head—not a real person, just a serious face, surrounded by billowing smoke and fire, making a lot of noise. With a thunderous roar, the Wizard demands to know how these four dare to challenge him. Here is the point: It's at this moment that Dorothy's dog runs over to a small room and pulls back a curtain, and what is revealed to us is a simple, flesh-and-blood man who has long been hiding behind a mask of power. He operates behind a curtain pulling levers, making smoke, fire, and noise. The result *looks* impressive but is only a facade. Even when exposed he roars, "Pay no attention to the man behind the curtain!"

The "Wizard" is in fact a power abuser. He controls a whole city with a facade that postures power and punishes people for noticing. In a kingdom where the problem was that the Wizard couldn't deliver, Dorothy and her crew became the problem for noticing there was a problem.

It is sad to think how often religious power-brokers control their spiritual kingdoms with power facades. They rain Bible verses on people about authority, submission, judgment, prosperity, or the end times. They penalize people for noticing that "the man behind the curtain" is just human, with no authenticity or authority at all.

As a maddening, last lesson from the story, after all is said and done the Wizard tells them, "You already have what you needed all along." They had risked life and limb for what they already had.

In too many Christian families and churches, Christians are told to jump through spiritual-performance hoops to earn God's approval—something they *already have* for free because of Jesus' death on the cross.

Conclusion

If false power and authority were the only elements of an abusive leader's facade, they would be easy to spot. In fact, some are. But there is another element to the facade that causes many, many people to suspend good judgment and spiritual discernment, to cross over from safe, true, life-giving spirituality into mere outward conformity.

We now turn our attention to that element—the misuse of *trust*.

hy·poc·ri·sy / *act of playing a part : feigning to be what one is not or to believe what one does not : false assumption of an appearance of virtue or religion.*

Another characteristic of false spiritual leaders is that they attempt to affect virtues or qualities they do not have. And they have a different set of rules for themselves than everyone else. They are hypocrites.

10

"You Can Trust Me"

Trust is not something that can be demanded or legislated. It is gained or lost on the basis of integrity and honesty. People who say what they mean and live consistently with their ideals are people you can trust, and more consistency is required of spiritual leaders as a demonstration of spiritual authenticity. Even if you don't agree with a person, or you don't affirm their ideals, there is something trustworthy about a man or woman who is "straight" with you. You know where you stand. It feels safe. It's even safe to disagree.

The image of the leader is still very clear in my mind's eye: Her smile was matronly, her eyes warm, her posture timid and submissive. The truth, however, was that behind the scenes she completely and bitterly undercut every aspect of ministry she could. She exuded evangelical honey on the outside—but facts slowly revealed that she was devious, contentious and full of gossip.

Eventually, when problems began to surface, she could not be confronted or challenged in any way. If you raised an issue, you were suspect, seen as a problem person who didn't "know how to trust."

In this little system trust was *expected*, even *required*. It was not something to be *earned*. How could anyone confront problems, then? How did you get to the truth? The leader always appeared so warm and gentle. Her whole demeanor seemed to emanate, "You can trust me—really." But her private pronouncements wounded people. What we were seeing was really "two people."

In Matthew 23 Jesus melts away the facade of spiritual "honey" to reveal two deadly aspects of false spiritual leadership: a double life (v. 3), and double-talk (vv. 16–18).

The Double Life of False Spiritual Leaders

Therefore all that they tell you, do and observe, but do not do according to their deeds; for they say things, and do not do them. (Matthew 23:3)

The verse begins with a curious statement: "... all that they tell you, do and observe." The obvious question is, if they are false teachers, why listen to *anything* they say? In fact, in Matthew 16:6, Jesus said of this same group, "Beware [literally: hold yourself back from] of the leaven of the Pharisees." Matthew 16:12 indicates the disciples understood that the leaven Jesus spoke of was the Pharisees' teaching, which was legalistic. He said it was wrong—"hold yourself back from it." Why then, in Matthew 23, would He tell them to do and observe all that they say?

The frightening fact is that even false leaders often use Scripture. The Pharisees and scribes knew the Bible better than anyone. They spent their lives memorizing it. But Jesus' directive in Matthew 23:3 simply means this: The degree to which even a false teacher uses Scripture faithfully, do it and observe it. The Word of God is good, even if the people who handle it are not. Don't throw out God's Word. But be wise about whom you receive it from and what they demand of you.

There is a common tendency among those who discover they have been victimized by spiritual abuse to throw the baby out with the bath water. No more Bible, no more God, no more Jesus—it's all a lie! I understand that reaction and I am sympathetic with it. But be careful. What Jesus is saying here means that even a spiritual abuse victim should continue to observe the truth, even as they are throwing out hypocrisy.

Most of us will never forget the images from several years back of Jimmy Swaggert as he appeared on Ted Koppel's program "Nightline," calling Jim Bakker "a cancer in the body of Christ." Jim Bakker at the time was under investigation for sexual misconduct and fraud. Swaggert's indignation seemed a bit strident at the time. It became hopelessly hypocritical when the reality of his own hidden life became known publicly. While in the midst of a sermon series that revealed the sins of Rahab the harlot, he had been visiting one himself. He was "saying but not doing." He had a double life.

The question that surfaces in the face of such sad events is, *why?* Not only why does it happen, but why does it seem to happen so often? Is there something fundamentally wrong in the church? What kind of dynamics are at work in us to produce such delusion and inconsistency? And, for each of us: *Are those dynamics at work in me?* We do not pretend to have all the answers to these questions, but perhaps we have one piece of the puzzle.

We believe that many leaders get trapped in what might be referred to as a spiritual "double-bind." It works like this: On the one hand, they may become involved in a behavior that they know to be wrong— for instance, going to a prostitute. The truth is, they probably really do despise it and desire to turn from it. The double-bind comes when the method they use to *prevent* the behavior sets them up instead to repeat it.

I do not believe that people who live double lives set out to do so. In most cases, they loathe what they do. Most of these people have struggled with a certain sin from their youth. And from their youth, they have desperately wanted to rid themselves of it. Then a problem occurs—let's say stress or overwork—and the willing spirit gets over-whelmed by a stressed-out will.

In most cases, the flesh's only method of dealing with and elimi-nating sinful behavior is to suppress it as tightly as possible. The most common suppression in the context of the church is to use external constraints—rules, injunctions, edicts, and prohibitions. Maybe if we preach loud enough, "resist the devil" long enough, try hard enough, scare people enough, go up to the altar enough, we'll somehow be able to hold this inner problem in check.

As an aside, we have encountered people who actually went into the ministry for the purpose of placing so many constraints on them-selves they could not "fall into sin." They are good people; they love God and hate sin—especially their own. But the only coping mech-anism they have ever employed to deal with their lust, or whatever sin, is to subdue it with their firm resolve. They neglect to deal with and heal from the wounds and motivations that lie beneath the surface of the external behaviors.

For someone in the ministry, this translates: "I'll be preaching every week about God's holiness and our need for self-control. The disci-pline of speaking it, and the subsequent need to model it, will help me 'keep the lid on it.' The ministry will provide for me the discipline that I need to keep the lid on. It will protect me. I'll preach about the wickedness of pornography on Sunday morning as a means of dealing with my addiction to it. Or I will preach about authority and submis-sion—from the pulpit of an independent, separatist church."

But does this "method" work to produce lust-free living or real inner holiness?

William Barclay, in doing a study on various sects of the Pharisees, came up with one category identified by him as "the bruised and bleeding Pharisees." Among all the sins that these Pharisees wanted to avoid in their quest for human holiness, they wanted to avoid lust the most. The way they could avoid lust was to never look upon a woman. They would put hoods over their heads in public and look at the ground, thereby avoiding any potential sinful distraction. But with hoods on their head and with eyes to the ground, they created another problem. They kept running into walls and falling down stairs! Thus the name "bruised and bleeding Pharisees."

What about this approach to "restraining" sin? It certainly speaks of good intentions. Yet Colossians 2 warns us graphically about defusing sin's power by purely external means:

> Why do you submit yourself to decrees, such as, "Do not handle, do not taste, do not touch!" . . . These are matters which have, to be sure, *the appearance of wisdom* in self-made religion and self-abasement and severe treatment of the body, but are of *no value* against fleshly indulgence (vv. 20–23)

If our method for dealing with the sin in our lives is to suppress it as tightly as we can, the chances are very high that one day the lid will blow.

External control for sin is no control at all. That's why Jesus said to the Pharisees in Matthew 23:25, "Woe to you, scribes and Pharisees, hypocrites! For you clean the outside of the cup and of the dish, but inside they are full of robbery and self-indulgence."

As pertaining to leaders who "appear" trustworthy, it is incredible how "shiny" they can look on Sunday morning. Any leader—ourselves included—can say all the right things and call people to all the right behaviors. But it is no good if that shiny veneer is simply a cover for an internal problem *that we know about, but will not handle by admitting we are powerless over it*. Jesus said, "I would that you would clean the inside of the cup and of the dish [deal with the real issues of your heart] so that the outside of it may become clean also."

If your method of dealing with sin is to tighten down the lid, put on an "in control" face, and polish the outside of the cup, it may work for a while. But eventually what's on the inside will explode to the surface. When it does, there will be casualties everywhere—especially if you're in the ministry.

What Is Our Only Hope?

At the very beginning of Jesus' ministry, He laid out principles of kingdom life that, if understood, unlock the door to real freedom and the spiritual life. He said new and wonderful things, as in Matthew 5:3, "Blessed are the broken." The language of brokenness is very easy to spot. It simply says, "I can't." Not, "I'm sad," "I'm sorry," "I feel bad"—but "I can't do it." "I need help." "I can't save myself!" When people finally realize that, they begin to develop a hunger for their only hope, which is God's saving grace. "For by grace you have been saved through faith; and that *not* of yourselves, it is the gift of God; not as a result of works, that no one should boast" (Ephesians 2:8–9).

We cannot save ourselves. Nor can we *sanctify* ourselves. When we are redeemed, we are given a brand new heart, implanted by the Holy Spirit. (See Ezekiel 37; Hebrews 11.) With that new heart comes a new desire to love God, to serve Him, to live holy. But the question still remains: How? The answer given all too often is, "Try hard, do more, really mean it this time." Interject the language of brokenness into that approach. "*I can't*: I can't subdue it, I can't control it, I am powerless." When we come to that terrifying realization—which we will do everything to avoid—we begin to develop a hunger for our only hope: sanctifying grace.

Here is a pattern worthy of note. The only way I could enter into salvation was to realize that I could *not* save myself. Liberty and life comes in hungering for and believing in a work of the Holy Spirit who would, by grace through faith, make me new. The pattern we need to see is that holy living comes the same way. Colossians 2:6 says, "As you therefore have received Christ Jesus the Lord, so walk in Him." The way we received Christ was by recognizing we "could not" establish our own righteousness. The way we walk is to recognize that we cannot on our own produce righteous behaviors—they come as God performs His spiritual work in us. This speaks of a lifelong reality of absolute dependence and faith.

"Blessed are those who mourn . . . " says Jesus in Matthew 5:4. The word "mourn" in the Greek is *penthos*. There are many Greek words describing various dimensions of grief and mourning. What captures our attention about this word *penthos* is that it specifically speaks of a visible external expression of internal pain. In other words, "to mourn" means "to show on the *outside* what is going on *inside*." Think about that. Isn't that different than "putting on the lid"? In fact, it is the complete opposite. Blessed are those who can show on the outside what is happening on the inside. Quit pretending you have no sadness, pain, fear, or sin, and get it out in the open where it can be dealt with, where God can really heal it. This is humility—and also integrity.

When there is no freedom to show on the outside what's on the inside, and no real brokenness, then there is no room for the grace of God. Sin has been pushed underground, and the result is a double life.

As we know, even our best spiritual leaders can become abusive of others while sadly leading double lives.

Double-Talk

The second manifestation of a lack of integrity is the use of "double-talk." Jesus refers to spiritual double-talk in Matthew 23:

> Woe to you, blind guides, who say, "Whoever swears by the temple, that is nothing; but whoever swears by the gold of the temple, he is obligated." You fools and blind men; which is more important, the gold, or the temple that sanctified the gold? And, "Whoever swears by the altar, that is nothing, but whoever swears by the offering upon it, he is obligated." (vv. 16–18)

To "swear" means to affirm with an oath that what I say is true. The reason that I am swearing is to get you to believe that what I say is true. "I swear," means, "You can absolutely trust me." In a court of law, in order to make sure that we are hearing the truth, we have people say, "I swear to tell the truth, the whole truth, and nothing but the truth, so help me God." And there are severe penalties for lying under such an oath.

A mark of false spiritual leadership is people who, in their effort to look good, *lie*. They don't talk straight. They rarely say what they mean, and because of that, some of their followers may actually sense that these people are hard to trust. In conversations, everything seems somehow veiled, or hidden, or else people are told they are not spiritual enough to understand teachings or decisions of the leaders. The leaders sound pious enough, even spiritual. But we are left with the vague sense that something is missing. They will give you the "right" answer, but rarely will you get the "real" answer. Everything has a double meaning. One result is that you cannot confront them or pin anything down. It will be hard to know where you stand.

In Matthew 5, Jesus did extensive teaching on the swearing of vows. He was giving a warning about making promises or vows, and attaching God's name to it so as to make it more believable. Matthew 5:34 says, "Don't make vows." Don't do it at all. In other words, stop using vows to gain people's trust. Just talk straight. Tell the truth. Say what you mean and mean what you say. People who talk straight are people you can trust. Even if you disagree with what they say, you'll know where you stand.

In Matthew 23:16 Jesus was uncovering obvious spiritual double-talk. These leaders would "swear by the temple" to get others to believe them. But when confronted later for not following through, they would never think of saying, "I'm sorry." Instead, they covered up with another lie.

We've all heard double-talk. We've all done double-talk. At best, it is a major irritation and a significant frustration. You can't get anywhere with someone who is speaking double-talk. It's like breaking a thermometer and trying to pick up the mercury. Meanings and motives keep slipping away. Double-talkers are, in slang terms, "slippery."

You Can't Seem to Ask the Question Right

In working with people, I have noticed that many feel they are excused from telling the truth, because the one confronting them "didn't ask the question just right." If you don't ask the question just right—meaning in anger, or in front of another—you do not get a straight answer.

Here is a segment of a conversation to demonstrate what we mean:

"You were asked to leave your church for sexually molesting a teenager. Have you gotten counseling?"

"Yes," was the reply. "I've been seeing someone for several months."

"Do they know how to address sexual issues?"

"Oh yes. They've had quite a bit of training."

"Then this person is a counselor?"

"You mean a *real* counselor?"

"Yes. Are they a counselor trained in sexual issues?"

"Well no, not really—it's a pastor. But he's read a lot of books. You know, I don't appreciate the way you're 'drilling' for answers."

Far more serious than the frustration of this kind of warped communication is the fact that this kind of lying destroys people. The reason why a person who is caught in abuse will lie and make bold promises is to gain your trust. Once they have convinced you they are safe again you can relax around them. And when you relax, they can do anything that they want, or get anything that they want. False spiritual leaders slowly stick in the spiritual knife and drain the life blood from you. This is why victims of abuse have a terrible time trusting people. They have tried that already.

As we reflect on the times that we have engaged in double-talk, part of the reason we did it is that at the time we needed to "look good" or be seen as "right." We did not want to lie; lying is wrong. But the need to look good or be right overcame the desire to speak truth. When this happens, the so-called right answer is not the real answer. We tell others what we think they want to hear, not what we really think. This is a lie. It is always a lie.

As pastors, we are also aware that there is a trap we can fall into, a pull toward speaking in double-talk. Many, if not most pastors receive messages from their congregation that signal: "Because you're the pastor, you need to look good, never struggle, always know the answer, and never be wrong." To succumb to those false "needs" is to let yourself become trapped in a double life and double-talk. How liberating to put all that down!

The fact is, no Christian always looks good. We struggle, and you struggle. Not one of us always knows the answer, and sometimes we are wrong. Embracing that reality sets us all free to say frightening, yet equally liberating things like:

"I'm sorry."

"I don't know."

"No."

"I disagree."

"You were right."

"I'm tired."

"I need help."

How many of us have come from families and churches where the unspoken rule was "How things look is more important than what is real"? Parents and spiritual leaders are supposed to be the best at reminding people to get their sense of acceptance and value from God. False leaders, however, turn to people's opinions and outward appearance as the sources of their validation. And real needs get lost in the shuffle.

11

Image Is Everything

But [the false leaders] do all their deeds to be noticed by men; for they broaden their phylacteries, and lengthen the tassels of their garments. And they love the place of honor at banquets, and the chief seats in the synagogues. (Matthew 23:5-6).

Some time ago, this verse came to mind as I (David speaking) was meeting in my office with a Bible college student who was doing an internship for a Pastoral Ministries course. The course was designed to teach people how to "act" like pastors.

As I questioned him regarding the essence of the class, it became clear that "image" was everything. How things looked was what really mattered. Simply *being* a pastor was clearly not enough—looking the part was the key. The better your image, the more successful you would be. Some of the advice given in this class went as follows: "Your wife and children must address you in public as 'pastor.' " This would serve to communicate reverence and respect for your position, which would be helpful in maintaining the proper image. "Sitting on the platform appropriately is vital. Wear the right socks, never cross your legs in such a way as to show people the soles of your shoes. Reveal your soul, never your soles." (Yes, they were really told this.)

More advice: "You're working on your car on your day off, and you discover that a trip to the parts store is necessary. Always change your clothes before you go out in public. Never let the people see you in a context other than pastoral dignity." Image is everything.

And the voice: "When you ascend the platform, remember—you are the voice of God. Sound like it." So we open our mouth and it sounds like we're playing a part, an actor on a stage. Material for stand-up comics.

Another tip for success: "Have the phone at church ring into your

home. When you answer it, always indicate, 'First Christian Church.' "
That way people will get the impression that you're at church all the
time, even though you are not.

Can you picture Jesus giving this kind of "training" to the disciples?
"Verily, verily, I say unto you, how you look is what really matters.
Create thou a good impression. Forget what I saith earlier to you
concerning having only one coat. Bringest thou two in case thou may-
est be seen in public by those who payeth their tithes in great measure.
And never, never let them smell the fish!" Do we really believe that
how we sit on the platform has the power to discredit the message
and short-circuit the power of God?

The real issue, for any Christian leader, is not, "How do I look or
how do I sound?" The real issue is, "Do I have a message from God
to give to the people? Do I have a 'fire' in my heart? Is the power and
reality of grace and the life of the Spirit pulsing through my veins?"

In Matthew 23 Jesus clearly exposes these image-conscious attitudes as consistent with false spiritual leadership and spiritual abuse:
"But they do all their deeds to be noticed by men." Posturing and
parading were the order of the day. Image was everything. The text
reveals a somewhat odd way to project this image, the "broadening
of phylacteries."

This practice was derived, in a twisted way, from Deuteronomy
6:5–8. There it says:

> And you shall love the Lord your God with all your heart and
> with all your soul and with all your might. And these words,
> which I am commanding you today, shall be on your heart . . .
> and you shall bind them as a sign on your hand and they shall
> be as frontals on your forehead.

The clear command of that text is to let your love for God be the
controlling factor—the binding force—upon what you do with your
hands and what you think in your mind.

The problem, however, was that over time what was meant *for* the
heart was no longer true *in* the heart. So it slipped to the outside,
becoming a way to look spiritual without being spiritual. They literally
put the commands of Deuteronomy into little boxes and tied them to
their wrists and foreheads. To "broaden them" simply meant to make
them bigger and more obvious. By doing this, they believed that people would think them utterly devoted to God.

Spiritual Show

The apostle Paul confronted this same kind of spiritual "show." In Galatians 6 he describes the Judaizers (false spiritual leaders) as "those who desire to make a good showing in the flesh" (v. 12). The essence of their spiritual life was to look good. They fell into the trap of believing that "how things look is what matters." The subtle danger of a system like this is that it becomes more important to look spiritual than to be spiritual. It's more important to look happy than to experience happiness. It's more important to have a marriage that looks strong than to have one that is strong.

Let's imagine for a moment that I am a pastor whose marriage is shaky. I'm altogether unhappy with my life, and my relationship with God dried up months ago. If I'm in a system where "how things look" is what matters, I can't possibly disclose any of the realities—it would not look good. So I pretend. My wife and I come through the door of the church arm in arm, slap on happy faces and sing with gusto. But the songs no longer have any meaning to us. We know deep in our spirit that something is radically wrong, but the thought of saying that out loud is terrifying. Everyone else here is healthy and happy. They could not possibly have the questions we have about God, or be struggling in their marriages, or ever get depressed. We are aware that something is wrong, but afraid of being ridiculed if we disclose the truth. We make a choice, and the choice is clear in a "how-things-look" system: You maintain a false image, and call it the abundant life.

The tragedy of all this is that you get *no* help for what's really going on in your life. God's amazing grace has no chance to touch and heal it, because it is kept hidden. When image is everything, when "how things look" is what matters, spiritual abuse is the next step, because you cannot help but demand performance from others when you are working so hard yourself.

The Place of Honor

Another mark that Jesus closely associates with the "image-is-everything" mentality is that you will need your performance affirmed by "the accolades of men." In Matthew 23, Jesus says, "And they love the place of honor at banquets and the chief seats in the synagogues." Their service to God is not at all for God; it is so they will be honored. If a spiritually abusive leader is not given a place of honor—is not publicly acknowledged—he or she will be sure that no one else is either. What prevails is jealousy and competition.

Meet Edythe

To bring perspective to the "place of honor," we quickly add that there is nothing at all wrong with being given that place.

Edythe Kiel was a woman at our church who, for years, quietly and faithfully served Jesus. We used to tease her that she was at church as much as most of the staff; but what she did, she did for free. One day we knew it was time to tell her how much we appreciated her untiring work. A surprise luncheon was decided upon. Edythe's primary area of responsibility was the kitchen, so nothing could go on there without her knowing. How could we keep this a surprise?

Knowing that no one could plan a premier banquet like Edythe could, we let her make the plans—but told her it was to be in honor of a guy named Ed. As usual, she was delighted to have a part in honoring someone special! We gave her a support staff, who set up the food. We ordered a cake that said, "Congratulations 'Ed.' "

On the day of the banquet, Edythe was standing in the doorway to the kitchen, beaming with delight, looking around for "Ed." Imagine her shock when the room full of people turned to her and said, "This whole thing is for *you*, Edythe!"

What a joy it was to eat that meal with her. By that time we had added onto the name "Ed" the letters *"ythe"* on the cake. What a gift it was for her to hear people one by one share what they loved about her. Edythe had the place of honor at that banquet, and she was supposed to have it. We gave it to her, and it was a very good thing.

Requiring Honor

The way you can spot a false system is that the leaders *require* the place of honor.

It is our belief that the less secure a leader is, the more important titles will be to him or her. The Pharisees, according to the text, had very little internal substance. All they had was the external polish. Clean but empty cups. When that is the case, it is very important that others notice the polished performance, since it is the sole source of value.

Several years ago, I was sitting in the living room of an accomplished medical professional. Gerald's home was beautiful, his children bright, his wife pleasant and accommodating. I sat there, shocked, as he began to reveal to me that the problem he had with our church was that there were so many "blue-collar types" who steadfastly called him "Gerry" instead of "Doctor." He felt like maybe it was time to leave the church.

In the early days of our ministry at Church of the Open Door, the services were transmitted into the nursery, for the benefit of the workers. Jeff's daughter Jesi was two years old at the time, and she recognized my voice on the speaker. With great delight at having solved an amazing mystery, she declared loudly, "That's Johnson!" A sweet lady working in the nursery gently picked her up, put her in her lap, and corrected her: "No, that's *Reverend* Johnson." Jesi became confused and looked again at the speaker. As she listened intently, the look of confusion was replaced by a look of determination as she declared a corrective of her own: "No—that's *Johnson!*" *Reverend* Johnson didn't work for this child, who knew me like a second daddy.

Maybe to some, the removal of recognition sounds disrespectful. The true issue is not whether you choose to use a title or not. The true issue is whether you *need* it—whether you have to have it. The Pharisees required it, and Jesus pointed out that this is one mark of a false spiritual leader.

True Leaders

The real heart of this issue is exposed by Jesus in Matthew 23:8–10:

> But do not be called Rabbi; for One is your Teacher, and you are all brothers. And do not call anyone on earth your father; for One is your Father, He who is in heaven. And do not be called leaders; for One is your Leader, that is, Christ.

Is Jesus giving us a legalistic rule—"Don't be called Rabbis . . . fathers . . . or leaders"? We believe it goes deeper than that. Its depth is made clear in the phrase, "One is your Teacher, One is your Father, One is your Leader." Let's take a closer look.

Rabbi is a title that speaks of knowledge and, more to the point, one who is a source of knowledge. The warning, therefore, is to not present yourself as the source of knowledge, for only One is our Teacher. *Leader* speaks of authority and direction. The warning is not to present yourself as the source of authority or as the director of another's life, for One is our Leader and that is Christ. *Father* speaks of source of life. The warning is not to present yourself as a source of life for anybody, for One is our Father—God alone.

Now, with that clarification, it becomes easier to distinguish the false shepherd from the genuine. Those who are *false* will present themselves as the source of all knowledge, authority, and life. For instance, those who are in a spiritually abusive system will often hear all other churches or Christian groups referred to as "dead." And when someone thinks of leaving, their leaders will not consider that leaving may actually be a growth step—the person will be warned that if they leave they will "die spiritually" or "fall away."

The *true* leaders will consistently and constantly point to Jesus. He is our primary source of knowledge, authority, direction and life. Jesus is the One who places us in certain bodies, where He knows we will grow closer to Him. And He is the One who will tell us to move on, when and if that is best for us.

Look for These "Marks"

To close this section, we refer to 1 Peter 5:1–5, as the apostle speaks of a true shepherd. Contrast Peter's list of characteristics with the characteristics we have examined:

Therefore, I exhort the elders among you, as your fellow elder and witness of the sufferings of Christ, and a partaker also of the glory that is to be revealed, shepherd the flock of God among you, exercising oversight not under compulsion, but voluntarily, according to the will of God; and not for sordid gain, but with eagerness; nor yet as lording it over those allotted to your charge, but proving to be examples to the flock. And when the Chief Shepherd appears, you will receive the unfading crown of glory. You younger men, likewise, be subject to your elders; and all of you, clothe yourselves with humility toward one another, for God is opposed to the proud, but gives grace to the humble.

How do we spot an image-oriented leader? Look for these marks:

- They operate from a false basis of authority.
- They lack integrity.
- They wear their spirituality on the outside.
- Spirituality is a put-on performance, an image they project.
- They require the recognition of people, calling it respect.
- They point to themselves as the primary source of knowledge, direction, authority, and life.

"You're out of order!" declared the elder leading the meeting. The church's young pastor had just told the assembly that he and his family were spiritually starving and financially dying. "We have important business to deal with here. You're not on the agenda."

In a spiritually abusive religious system, the mundane becomes essential, the vital trivial. And the real needs of real people are neglected for the sake of "agendas."

12

Straining Gnats, Swallowing Camels

Don has been a Christian for many years. For most of that time he was involved quite extensively in a variety of ministries. About three years ago Don began to find that he had major problems in his relationship with God. His spirituality was tiring and dry. God seemed silent and distant.

Consequently, he sought help and support from a number of different resources, including a conference we present at Church of the Open Door called "Breaking the Silence." This is a five-day workshop that helps people come to grips with shame and related issues like addiction, emotional abandonment and neglect, sexual abuse and spiritual abuse.

Don's birthday occurred during the week he was at the conference and he received a number of cards. One of them was from his father. When Don was born his dad was a preacher who pastored three small churches. In the card, Don's dad mentioned that he had been going over an old diary and found the entry from the day of Don's birth, which happened to be a Sunday. Then he wrote, "I had to miss two church services that day. You sure picked a bad time to be born."

It was as if a door of understanding opened in Don's soul. Suddenly, fifty years of believing that he was not important, just an interruption in the lives of others, made sense. Don finally had the words to explain the uncomfortable sense of being in the way, of not counting. Sadness, grief, and anger flooded over him as he got in touch with what it feels like to always come in second to "the ministry."

Upside-Down Spirituality

Don's father suffered from what we would call *inverted spiritual values*. He evidently valued leading a group of Christians in "worship" more than He valued standing before God in joy, receiving into his hands a flesh-and-blood miracle. A ritual, a meeting was more important than a new life—than life itself. Don had suffered from one form of a minister's trying to draw life and fulfillment from the wrong source. Recently, we heard about another scenario, different yet also incredibly damaging.

It was no longer the latest evangelical scuttle. This was the local ten o'clock news. The face on the TV screen was a familiar one: a respected pillar in the community, the pastor of a large church. Conservative, evangelical, fundamental. He'd been there fifteen years, and it was under his leadership that the church grew to prominence.

He was being prosecuted for sexually molesting a young adolescent boy. It couldn't be true! The boy must have been rejected in some way, and now this was his means of getting revenge. But it was true. And after the first revelation there came more, and then more. A crack had opened the wall of secrecy and now the water of truth, dammed up for fourteen years, was pouring out for all to see.

Among the disclosures that followed were these troubling realities, which are important for us to examine: First, many of the elders had knowledge of this behavior—certainly not its extent, but its presence. Second, a conscious choice was made to keep it quiet in hopes it would simply blow over. "It's not that big a deal." "We don't want to damage the ministry." Both were lies. It was a big deal; the ministry was already damaged.

What's ironic, even tragic, about this choice to ignore devastating transgressions was how firm this church was known to stand on matters of far less consequence. For instance, much was made over issues such as proper attire in church. Communion stewards were strictly instructed that if they did not wear suitcoat and tie they would be barred from serving communion.

What's revealed by such upside-down values? While strong stands were being taken on issues of little or no spiritual significance, issues of grave consequence were being ignored. Jesus called this "straining gnats and swallowing camels."

This focus on the picayune, the kind of detail that actually *distracts* from real issues, is another mark of an abusive spiritual system.

Jesus says in Matthew 23:

Woe to you, scribes and Pharisees, hypocrites! For you tithe mint and dill and cummin, and have neglected the weightier provisions of the law: justice and mercy and faithfulness; but these are the things you should have done without neglecting the others. You blind guides, who strain out a gnat and swallow a camel! (vv. 23–24)

The issue Jesus raises is one of inverted spiritual values. In systems like this, the *insignificant* becomes the *significant*, and the significant becomes insignificant. The irrelevant becomes paramount, and the trivial becomes vital.

The spiritually impotent Pharisees manifested their spiritual disease by carefully tithing (giving 10 percent to God), even from their stores of little seeds, like mint, dill and cummin. But matters like justice, mercy, and faithfulness were ignored. That is evidence of inverted spiritual values.

Of Gnats and Camels

In an attempt to make sure the confrontation is clear, Jesus gives an illustration: "You blind guides, who strain out a gnat and swallow a camel!" (v. 24). In the mind of a Jew, the picture would be understood clearly. Under Levitical law, both the camel and the gnat were considered ceremonially unclean. Obviously, it was easier to avoid swallowing a camel than a gnat. (Generally, if you swallowed a camel you'd notice!)

Gnats were a tougher matter. You had to work to avoid them. Bugs were everywhere. In the making of wine, for instance, there was no refrigeration, no filtering system, and the pressing of grapes was done by foot in large, open vats. A significant number of "unclean" guests made their way into the wine. Still pretending they could avoid *any* unclean intrusion, the Pharisees sifted their wine through their teeth and then picked out the bugs with their fingers. The meaning of Jesus' confrontation could not be lost on them. "You put incredible amounts of energy into things of little consequence (dill, mint and cummin), but you swallow the camel (immorality, injustice, lying, hypocrisy). You have inverted spiritual values."

What is the meaning in this for us today? Again and again we see that the issue of inverted spiritual values is alive and well in the church. Many have grown up in churches that teach: Never let wine touch your lips, never play cards (not even "Rook"), never dance, never go to movies, and never smoke. To avoid some behaviors may in fact be a very good thing to do. But what if those same externally "clean" people are full of bitterness, anger and malice? In the church where I (David speaking) grew up, we very carefully monitored external behaviors, carefully sifting out even such "evils" as bowling. I used to wonder why bowling was so evil, while being a dried-up old sourpuss was okay. Having long hair, for men, was definitely a sign that you were damned to hell, but malicious gossip was no big deal. In short, we took our religious behaviors very seriously— even when they got ridiculous.

"El's Bells"

It was a tradition in our church, for instance, that every Christmas Eve Eleanor would play "the bells." Eleanor was the church organist and she took herself and her bells—cowbells they were—very seriously. The cowbells were all different sizes for different notes, and were set on a table covered in red satin. She wore a black dressy suit, white gloves and stood very erect, looking like she would snap in half if she bent over too far. As she began playing, an auspicious hush would fall over the crowd, all of us showing the cowbells their proper respect.

All, that is, except my brother Steve and me. We were little boys, and to our way of thinking this harmless, stiff-backed lady playing "Away in the Manger" with cowbells was nothing short of *roll-in-the-aisles* hysterical. As we got a little older and a little more "worldly," we began to affectionately refer to the event as "El's Bells." In our own way, it really *was* a joyous holiday occasion. Eleanor would begin to play; my brother and I would get the giggles; my mother would pinch us on the leg until we bruised. It happened every Christmas.

One particular Christmas, an event occurred that will go down in the annals of bell-playing history. I was nine years old and my brother was seven. "El's Bells" had begun—and so had we. We did our best, as always, to stifle our levity—but it was no use. Even my mother's patented "Finger Nail Torture" didn't help.

There was a lady sitting right in front of us, in "her pew," the same one she occupied every Sunday. I don't remember her name, just her demeanor. She was not a pleasant person. At the end of the service she spun around to confront my brother and me for our giggling with a face like a courthouse gargoyle. In a shrill voice she blurted a question that trailed into the ozone octaves, and meant to shame us: *"Are you saaaaaaaaaved?"*

I remember being afraid. Could laughing at "El's Bells" really put my salvation up for grabs? Would God pull back His acceptance of me because I laughed in church? Nine year-old boys wonder and worry about such things.

As time passed, of course, I was able to sort out the truth. My brother and I were probably inappropriate. We probably should have shown more respect. God knows that we honestly tried. But in her rage, the lady in front of us had picked out the meanest, scariest thing she could think of to say and she slashed us with it. Her purpose was to silence and punish, and it worked. Its effect, however, was short-lived. I decided that if Jesus had heard cowbells in the temple playing "Away in the Manger," He would have gotten the giggles too.

Our point in all of this is to help others do some important spiritual "sorting." We can all be guilty of "straining gnats and swallowing camels," and of focusing on insignificant *behaviors* while the important *souls* of people are ignored or even damaged.

Let's take a look at a brief list of modern "bugaboos" among Christians that can take the place of more significant concerns.

A Contemporary List

Musical evils

While attending a Christian college, the pastor of worship at our church had a music professor who constantly harped on the evils of contemporary Christian music. He made it clear that a person's singing style was a spiritual issue. There is what he called a "sensual vibrato" that is particularly evil. And of course this assumes there is also a kind of vibrato God particularly likes. According to this man God only likes traditional, classical music.

As an aside, while this respected teacher was decrying the evils of "sensual vibrato," he was giving full-body massages to his female student assistants on his office floor. Of course not all who dislike or decry contemporary music are as blind as this man, and for some the avoidance of *any* music that triggers bad associations is even good. But eventually, we must face and deal with whatever is on the inside of our "spiritual cup"—in this man's case, at least, a blindness about what prompts lust.

Obeying the laws of the land

This sounds almost too silly, but it's true. There was a Christian leader who never drove over 55 mph—and the reason people knew was because he told them. To him it was a spiritual issue, one from which he drew great pride. To him, it demonstrated spirituality because he was obeying the Bible's decree to submit ourselves to every authority, including the civil government. He would rail against unlawful Christians who pushed the speed limit. They were "poor witnesses."

The problem was that this same elder was sleeping with his best friend's wife. He was breaking not only God's Law, but the "laws" of common friendship that exist in even non-Christian relationships.

When all is said and done, abusive spirituality is more interested in supporting *doctrines* (spiritual mindsets, mentalities, ways of viewing God) than in supporting *people*. It is not interested in learning the true conditions in which God builds a living relationship with people—by grace, for free, to become a wellspring of inner spiritual resource. For God himself is interested in men and women finding the right way to connect with and draw life from Him.

Real Christians Dance

I want to close this chapter by completing the story of Don, whose birth had "intruded" upon his father's ministry, and who had grown up believing systems were more important than people. My wife and I recently received an invitation to a square dance being held in Don's honor. At the bottom of the invitation was a note from Don's wife that said, "There is a story behind this. We'll tell you about it at the dance."

Here is the story, as we heard it:

After Don realized that he'd been rejected in favor of "the ministry," he began a process of recovery from spiritual abuse. He saw a counselor on a regular basis to sort out the hurt and anger of his childhood, and to disentangle it from his sense of dryness with God. One day, Don and the counselor were talking about Don's complete aversion to reading the Bible. In the course of that session he realized that the Bible was, in a sense, an "idol" to his father. In other words, his father tried to gain his value and acceptance from preaching God's Word, instead of receiving value and acceptance as a gift from God himself.

This resulted in a son who was neglected, one who felt unimportant to God and, therefore, resentful.

"What do you think I should do?" Don asked the counselor.

"What did they do with idols in the Old Testament?" the man replied.

"Well . . . I guess they burned them," Don finally answered.

"Well?" replied the counselor.

Though this will shock many Christians, Don burned his Bibles. But we hasten to add that the birthday celebration brought the delightful news that Don had, eventually, gone out and bought a new Bible, all on his own, because he had come to a new inner hunger for God's Word that was real and not out of obligation. It was as if in order to have his own relationship with God, he had to reject the god of his father.

Don also became involved in a group for adult children of pastors, missionaries, etc. who had been abused or neglected "in the name of God." And not long before Don's birthday, a woman in the group mailed him a poem entitled *God Danced*. It seems the Holy Spirit used the poem to say to Don: "God danced the day you were born." Now Don had this new Bible to symbolize his own relationship with God. And in it he read Psalm 139, especially verses 13–16:

> Thou didst form my inward parts; Thou didst weave me in my mother's womb. I will give thanks to Thee, for I am fearfully and wonderfully made; wonderful are Thy works, and my soul knows it very well. My frame was not hidden from Thee, when I was made in secret, and skillfully wrought in the depths of the earth. Thine eyes have seen my unformed substance; and in Thy book they were all written, the days that were ordained for me, when as yet there was not one of them.

Don realized that God was "dancing" about him *before* he was even born. Ephesians 1:4 also said to him, "[God] chose us in Him before the foundation of the world." Not just before Don was born, but before the world was made.

So when we received the invitation to Don's birthday square dance, we knew something had changed in Don's heart. He had finally heard the eternal "Yes!" thundering from the Father's heart from the beginning of time. Can you imagine what it looks like, what it feels like, for fifty years of overdue celebration to finally break loose?

Don had learned, at last, that God is for people, not religious systems.

Another tendency of spiritually abusive leaders is that they add to the burdens of those who follow. Instead of grace and mercy to help in time of need, they offer religion. Whatever happened to "My load is light and my yoke is easy"? Find out in this chapter.

13

The Weight of Religion

Some time ago someone mailed me a bulletin from a large church in the southeastern U.S. This "test" was on page one:

Check Yourself

If people were like you:

- Would they be in Sunday School next Sunday?
- Would they be on time?
- Would they bring a Bible?
- Would they have studied the lesson?
- Would they bring an offering?
- Would they attend the preaching service?
- Would they make an effort to worship during the service?
- Would they bring someone with them?
- Would they invite a new member or visitor?

Give yourself 10 points for every question that you could answer "yes." If your score is 100—you are a perfect example! If 90—you're just about right; 80—you're slipping; 70—watch your step; 60—you're an emergency case.

Six successful Sundays in Sunday School continues this Sunday. Be there!

After taking this test, is your spiritual burden heavier, or lighter? Do you feel more sensitive to the voice of the Holy Spirit, or to the pressure of this pastor?

The apostle Paul went to war over spiritual scoring systems, as we read in Galatians 5: "It was for freedom that Christ set us free; therefore keep standing firm and do not be subject again to a yoke of slavery"

(v. 1). But how many of us have been taught to fear "too much grace"? How many of us suffer from a fear that if we take off the "yoke" of spiritual performance and release the load of guilt and pressure, what in the world will restrain sin? What's going to motivate people to obey God?

We believe the Holy Spirit of God who lives *in* them is fully able to do that. We believe that God is capable of motivating a person to live an obedient life. As Paul said in Philippians 1:6, "For I am confident of this very thing, that He who began a good work in you will perfect it." And again in Philippians 2:13, "For it is God who is at work in you, both to will and to work for His good pleasure." Galatians 5:16 also says, "But I say, walk by the Spirit, and you will not carry out the desire of the flesh."

Backlash

When we first began to preach this message at Church of the Open Door, people got very nervous. "This will never work," some said. "If we take the external pressures off people and rely on an internal work of the Holy Spirit, we'll have chaos."

And in fact, when we took off the external manipulations, some people did move joyfully into sin. That is, they began to do what was in their heart to do all along. Make no mistake, that is painful to watch. But there is a benefit to seeing that: Now you know you are dealing with a person who has an unredeemed heart.

Several years ago (David speaking), I had in my office the concerned mother of a teenaged boy. She came to ask me to get her son to listen to different music, go to different places, and to have different friends. At one point she blurted, "I want you to get him to stand up for what he believes."

I responded to her by saying, "What you need to understand is that he already is! Now, if you want me to pray that God breaks his heart and gives him a new one, I'll do that. If you want me to talk to him about his need for something different *inside*, I'll do that! But if you want me to pressure him to simply 'behave,' I won't do that. I know *you'd* feel better, because he would look good. But all we'd have is a shined up Pharisee, going straight to hell."

Either God's Word is true or it is not. Truly redeemed people *have* a new heart. They have the life of Christ *in* them by the resident Holy Spirit. They desire to follow and obey God. That doesn't mean they always do. Sometimes Christians stumble—even badly. But their hearts hunger for God. His law of life has been written on the inside (Hebrews 10:16).

In Matthew 23, we read about Jesus' encounter with the spiritually abusive leaders of his day, men who relied on external pressures while ignoring urgent matters of the heart. They, like all off-target spiritual leaders through the ages, were trying to control people's behavior by demanding external religious performances. Of these leaders—"false guides" He called them—Jesus said, "They tie up heavy loads and put them on men's shoulders. . ." (Matthew 23:4, NIV).

In using this imagery, Jesus was calling forth a very sad-comic sight, so common in those days. His listeners would have known at once what he was getting at; they would have gotten the picture. Permit us a moment to paint it for you.

The first century version of a 4-wheel-drive truck was a poor beast of burden known as the donkey. The primary function of a donkey was to carry things. A common practice in Palestine at the time of Christ was to load these animals with so many goods that the animal itself could not be seen. The donkey would quite literally disappear under the load.

That is the unhappy message Jesus wanted to call forth when He likened abusive leaders to donkey handlers, spiritual switch in hand, serving only to put more weight upon the people and keep them moving down the road. The spiritual imagery is not only graphic, but it strikes at the heart of what many people have experienced in the church. Under an overwhelming load of false guilt and religious performance, the person underneath that load feels as though their personhood and their own identity in Christ is about to disappear.

On the other hand, the function of a true shepherd is to remove the load of external performances, and help people discover the freedom and joy of their new identity in Christ. It's true that when some people strip it all away, they discover they don't know God and never did. The only thing keeping them in line was the weight of the religious load. Others, however, take the load off and discover the life of God in them for the first time. They begin to move through life and do the things they do by promptings and direction of the Spirit.

People have experienced this phenomenon in the church since it began. Let's look at this more closely.

"Salvation is not free" or "Salvation is free, but to live as a Christian you have to pay . . ."

"Works" have long been a problem for many in the church. Paul had performed so many righteous acts as a Pharisee trying to be holy that he developed acute spiritual perception that told him the moment a body of believers was in danger of forgetting that God's gift of salvation was free. Let's consider two ways a "spiritual work for spiritual pay" mentality affects the church today.

First is the mentality that regardless of what the Bible says, our church tradition tells us we must *work for our salvation*.

A spiritual load is placed upon the people by a theology that says: "God is adding up all your good behaviors and all your bad behaviors. If, in the end, the good outweighs the bad, He might accept you into His heaven." The object, then, is to pile up more good than bad. But note that in this system you always carry the load of *both* your good and bad behaviors. Nothing ever *removes the weight of sin*; the strong arm of grace is never extended. As Jesus says in Matthew 23: "[These false leaders] are unwilling to move [the load of sin] with so much as a finger" (v. 4). The only hope you have in this system is that your good behaviors outweigh your bad—but the operative word here is "weigh." You carry it all.

In a works-righteousness system, if you stumble under the load you are carrying, the ministry you will receive will not be mercy and grace. You will not hear Matthew 5:3: "Blessed are the poor in spirit"— that is, "Blessed are those who recognize they *can't* carry the load,"— "for theirs is the kingdom of heaven." Rather, you will be encouraged to "try a little harder" and "do a little more." In some cases you may be shamed for "not being committed enough."

Second, there is performance-based Christianity, a most common malady among Christians. It manifests itself this way. After having understood the truth of Ephesians 2:8–9—"For by grace you have been saved . . ."—and having had the load of sin removed for salvation, we then lay on a load of personal performance for sanctification, service, and to receive further blessings.

It works something like this. We are very careful to help people understand that Jesus is their only hope for salvation. "*He* saved us, not on the basis of deeds which we have done in righteousness, but according to *His* mercy" (Titus 3:5). But for successful Christian living, we give the same message they had to reject in order to get saved. "Just do it." "Try hard." "Do more." "It's up to you." We pile up a load of expectations, regulations, formulas and rules. Almost without noticing, we begin to live the same way we did before we met Jesus, hoping that with all our effort we will someday, some way, measure up. But we never do measure up; we continue to carry the load and we call it "the abundant life."

This dynamic is really not that hard to spot. In a performance-based system, you will be the bearer of the burden. In a grace-based system, you will be constantly directed to Jesus as your only hope, encouraged to rest in Him as your only source of life and power.

What About the People?

This song, by Steve Taylor, accurately describes the plight of the person whose real human needs, or whose relationship with God, is violated for the sake of making a system look good.

I Want to Be a Clone[1]

1. I'd gone through so much other stuff
   That walking down the aisle was tough,
   Now I know it's not enough.
   I want to be a clone.
   I asked the Lord into my heart.
   They said, "This is the way to start,
   Now you've got to play the part."
   I want to be a clone.

Chorus:
   Be a clone and kiss conviction good-night.
   "Cloneliness" is next to godliness—right?
   I'm grateful that they showed the way,
   'Cause I could never know the way
   To serve Him on my own.
   I want to be a clone.

2. They told me that I'd fall away
   Unless I followed what they say.
   "Who needs the Bible anyway?"
   I want to be a clone.
   Their language it was new to me,
   But "Christianese" got through to me.
   Now I can speak it fluently.
   I want to be a clone.

3. So now I see the whole design,
   My church is an assembly line.
   My parts are there, I'm feeling "fine."

---

[1]From the song "I Want to Be a Clone," written by Steve Taylor, © 1983 Birdwing Music/ Music Services/Cherry Lane Music Publishing Co. All rights controlled and administered by Sparrow Corporation, Box 5010, Brentwood, TN 37024. All rights reserved. International copyrights secured. Reprinted by special permission.

I want to be a clone.
I've learned enough to stay afloat,
But not so much to rock the boat.
I'm glad they shoved it down my throat.
I want to be a clone.

Misguided shepherds add weight to the spiritual loads of those who follow. And in the process, people's identities get lost in the sea of religious packaging.

Conclusion

We believe that "amazing grace" really works. When people experience the "truth that sets you free" their lives change from the inside out. They begin to give of their financial resources because God by His Spirit really is producing gratitude or conviction in their heart. It is *grace giving*, not merely responding to a rule.

Suddenly their approach to Bible study changes. No longer do they read God's Word to prove to Him they are good. That load has been removed. Now, they begin to sound like Jeremiah, who said, "Thy words were found and I ate them, and Thy words became for me a joy and the delight of my heart" (Jeremiah 15:16).

As we have seen earlier, however, the goal of spiritually abusive systems is primarily to call people in and keep them in, whether or not they are finding life there. We believe that this is no small matter, but a dynamic that has serious, sometimes even eternal, implications.

What a scene it must have been that day at the temple. How could a temple, with tables falling, dust flying, doves flapping and priests fleeing, be considered "cleansed"? And just why was Jesus so angry at the chief priests and vendors?

This wasn't about having a garage sale in the church basement. It was about perverting the purpose of God's house. Instead of finding free access to God and His grace, people had to pay and perform. And even then they couldn't get to God. Have you ever felt that way?

14

"No Admittance"

To this point, some readers will have identified religious environments with the characteristics described here, and acknowledge the effects—but simply shrug it off. "Oh sure, I've seen all that in our church, but it's no big deal. We're all on the same team." But what we are describing is no small matter.

How misguided it is to teach that closeness to God is a function of religious performance, not a gift! What an irony to demand "formula" living that will make people "good enough" to live close to Emmanuel, "God with us." It is this outrage that Jesus addressed in Matthew 23:

> "But woe to you, scribes and Pharisees, hypocrites, because you shut off the kingdom of heaven from men; for you do not enter in yourselves, nor do you allow those who are entering to go in." (v. 13)

Before we delve into the nuances of this verse, we must be aware of the textual flow of the twelve verses that come before and lead into this strong denunciation of pharisaical practice. As we have touched on earlier, Jesus was revealing the fundamental characteristics of false spiritual leaders. It was His profile of spiritual abusers. We have seen so far that such leaders, knowingly or unknowingly, have:

- a false basis of authority (v. 2);
- a double life, "They say but do not" (v. 3);
- a habit of placing heavy loads on people (v. 4);
- a tendency to wear religion on the outside so as to win the accolades of men (v. 6–10).

As we come to verse 13, it is as if Jesus shifts His confrontation into a higher gear. In this section, He goes beyond simply identifying characteristics and describes the impacts of such people. We believe that one reason for this intensifying tone is to prevent us from minimizing the danger.

In verse 3, Jesus categorically states that this *is* an important matter, not simply a question of normal, allowable variances in ministry style. We are dealing here with issues that "shut off the kingdom of heaven" from people. This is a matter we must seriously explore.

Slamming the Door to God's Rulership

To "shut off" in the Greek literally means "to slam the door in the face of, and to make entry impossible." In a performance-oriented setting, what is impossible is entry into God's kingdom—that is, into the true *rule* of God. If people are shut out from the possibility of experiencing the reign and rule of God in their lives, this is a serious matter indeed.

Spiritually abusive systems do not shut people out from synagogues, temples—or, in our Christian context, from churches or Bible studies. On the contrary, systems like this spend great energy trying to get people to *come* (as we'll see in the next chapter). Consequently, people may first experience fellowship and a sense of being "right with God." But in the context of a false authority, increasing loads, external performance, and religious pride, it is unlikely that the experience of joyful liberty under God's reign will continue.

Consider this: Is it possible to grow up in the church, do all the "do's," don't do the "don'ts," know all the doctrine—and still not enter into the kingdom? What a tragedy to spend a lifetime *around* religion and never to have experienced the reality of Christ alive in and among us! Such is the danger in a spiritually abusive system. We dare not minimize this. We must all examine whether we are offering people life in the Spirit only to substitute something far less when they have accepted the invitation.

The "Bait-and-Switch"

Among the most common tricks in an unscrupulous businessperson's bag is something known as the "bait and switch." We may be enticed by a promise of pleasure or wealth with "the bait," but when we reach for the promised object, the switch takes place and we get only a facsimile of what we reached for, not at all the real thing. A form of this very thing is what takes place in spiritually abusive systems.

The victim, in this case, is the man or woman looking for meaning in life. More than that, they are looking for God. They have tried everything the world has to offer and they are still empty inside. They need more. The bait in a spiritually abusive system is the promise of a relationship with God, rest for the soul, forgiveness of sins, and nothing less than a brand-new identity in Christ Jesus. And best of all, it's *free*. It comes by grace through faith.

The switch takes place when, upon arriving, we receive a heavy load of new rules and external performances to live up to. We still hear words and sing songs about grace and life, but there seems so little of the genuine article. There is no life-giving *reign* of God, only a substitute God who suddenly demands a great deal of activity from us to "prove" we are "worthy servants." In fact, God-talk is used to drive people. We end up with a facsimile of what we came for. How did the "bait and switch" take place?

Matthew 23:13 reveals more about this dynamic in the statement "nor do you allow those who are entering [the kingdom] to go in." Here, Jesus indicates that the ones who are being denied access to the kingdom are not rebellious God-rejectors. They are the *God-seekers*. They are the ones responding to God's own prompting to find Him, to "enter in." In their attempt to enter in, they do the obvious thing: they go to church. But when they get to church (and receive an enthusiastic welcome), they do not find God and grace and light and life. They come under a false basis of authority, heavy weights of legalistic load-carrying, and external performance with no internal reality. They get a "form of godliness void of power" (2 Timothy 3:5).

Millions of people have experienced church, or some form of Christianity. But if that experience came in the context described in Matthew 23, they may have never experienced the freeing, life-giving reign of God. We must never forget that there is a significant difference between the church and the kingdom. For some, it may even be the difference between life and death, entering in and being shut off, heaven and hell.

An Imaginary Journey

A graphic illustration of Jesus' attitude toward such systems is found in Matthew 21, where we see Him cleanse the temple. Let's set the scene. It is the Passover in Jerusalem. Jews from all over the world, desiring to meet with God and be obedient to His commands, have made the pilgrimage to the holy city. Perhaps it will be easier to understand Jesus' actions if we dramatize the experience of one father as he arrives with his family in Jerusalem:

"I was feeling more excitement and anticipation this year than in other years. For the first time, all the children could really understand what is going on. We had already noticed a simple faith in them, and they have a yearning for the truth of God that I have not seen before. Surely, we thought, the place to fan that flame is at the temple in Jerusalem.

"I remember looking at them with their yearling lamb. For months they had cared for him, and he became to them a cherished pet— though he was to be our family's sacrifice. The children had chosen to raise the lamb themselves. This sacrifice was clearly a gesture from their hearts.

"When we came into Jerusalem there were two imposing images that I shall never forget.

"First, the temple itself, its silent stones keeping us away from the holy presence of God. Courtyards within courtyards, allowing fewer and fewer people near to the Holy of Holies. All could enter into the outer courtyard, the place of the Gentiles. Beyond that was an imposing door and another courtyard. Into this courtyard, only we Jewish men could go—no Gentiles, no women, no children. There were six ascending courtyards in all. Each of them excluded a few more people until, at the top of the temple mount, stood the final court. This was the Holy of Holies. Into that place only the high priest could dare to venture, and only once a year, on the Day of Atonement.

"As I stood with my family in the outer court, I felt small and insignificant. I want to know God. I think I love God. But will I ever be acceptable in His sight? This I do not know. Only the religious leaders can say.

"But then I was struck with the second imposing image—the Bazaar of Annas.

"The bazaar was created by the former high priest, Annas, to provide pilgrims with all the necessary implements of worship. Space in the courtyard was rented to chosen vendors, who set up shop in small booths. Each booth provided animals for sacrifice and implements for cleansing. In addition, there were many religious trinkets you could buy to prove devotion. The prices were very, very high. A lamb purchased at the temple could cost ten times the market value.

"We were taught by the rabbis not to question whether this bazaar really did provide a necessary service. After all, people could lose their sacrifice on the long journey or forget some necessary tool and purchase it here.

"Then I saw what was called the 'booth of approval,' manned by one of the strictest of the Pharisees. Before we could offer our family's lamb for sacrifice it had to be 'approved.'

"We stood in a long line, nervously waiting for our lamb to be inspected. Our disappointment rose as it became clear that most of the people's offerings were being rejected. 'Not good enough.' 'Not clean enough.' 'Not big enough.' By the time our turn came, I knew the verdict and I was right: 'Rejected.'

" 'Go to one of the vendors' booths,' we were told. 'There you can purchase a lamb pre-approved for sacrifice. You don't even have to come back here for approval. They can take care of all your needs right there.'

"My heart sank. The children were confused. What about our lamb? What about our sacrifice? Doesn't God care about that? How do *we* get to God? I suppose we just have to follow the rules. After all, we are in the temple. True, something feels wrong in all this—but this is God's House. It says so, right on the sign outside.

"I supposed we should just pick a vendor's booth and get on with it—which one did not seem to matter much. They all had a little different sales-pitch, but basically the same merchandise was available. We finally settled on a vendor because he looked friendly. He quickly sold us a lamb at ten times its real value. Then he proceeded to inform us of the other necessary implements for "proper" worship that we did not know of. Wanting to show our true love for God, we paid all the fees.

"But there was a serious problem at the end of the day. It was simply this: We never knew if we were pleasing to *God*—or just to the religious leaders. It seemed that the kingdom of heaven was too far beyond our reach. . . ."

Jesus Responds

This scene is what Jesus saw when He entered the temple that day. This is why He turned over the tables in a righteous rage. The temple designed by God to be a place where men and women could meet with God—"My house shall be called a House of Prayer" (v. 13)—had become a place where people were abused in the name of

God. He declared: "But you have made it a den of thieves" (v. 13b). The tragic truth was that in this system, the least likely place to meet with God would be in the temple.

The unhappy news is that, for many, this is still a reality today. There are people longing for God, and they hope that the logical place to discover the truth about God is in a place that claims to have it— the church. But when they go, all too often what they discover is a system that gives them more work to do in order to be "close" to God.

Sometimes tired out Christians leave church and give up on God altogether. Sometimes they stay, though, hoping things will change. They lower their expectations. They decide that this is as good as it gets. ("No church is perfect. And all our friends are here. . . .") But they pay and pay and pay, and rarely experience the kingdom—the true reign of God.

Jesus warns all of us who are spiritual leaders today: Woe to you, if you shut off the kingdom of heaven from men.

But there is always hope beyond the warning. *Jesus fights for us*, against all empty religious performance—even our own particular denominational brands. Picture Jesus, standing in the courtyard of the Gentiles, standing against a powerful religious system that presumes to speak for God. He is breaking the "can't-talk" rule that silences honesty and allows the system to perpetuate itself. He breaks the cycle of abuse. When He did, during His earthly life, it so enraged the religious pretenders that they nailed Him to a cross. It was, in fact, three days after the cleansing of the temple that they executed Him.

Did Jesus know what was coming? Do you think He knew that these words of His would be the "last straw"? That it would cost Him His life? We think He did, and it makes us grateful. It makes us want to worship. It makes us want to do what He did, and say what He said. It makes us look at our lives and our ministry and ask the question: *Are we door-openers, or door-closers?*

Another fact that lies beyond Jesus' warning not to rely on performance but to trust in God's grace is this: When we do, people are set free and healed. The poor, blind, lame and others were right in the middle of the violent explosion when Jesus turned over the tables in the temple (Matthew 21:12–16). And it was then, when they saw His authenticity, that a most wondrous event happened. "And the blind and the lame came to Him in the temple and He healed them" (v. 14). With the false system overturned—with feathers filling the air from scurrying doves, and coins clanging and scattering across the floor as the moneychangers run for cover—the lame and the blind come to

Him. The Pharisees were afraid of Him, but these wounded people knew Jesus was safe, approachable. They knew He was fighting for them, and they came for His touch.

There is a serious reminder for us in this. Before Jesus cleared the temple, blind and lame people were a hindrance to its operation. They were beggars, always in the way, a problem to be pushed into corners, out of the way. Today, too many hurting people in a church are "bad public relations." But when Jesus turned over the tables, the hurting were no longer a hindrance to the operation of the temple, they *were* the operation of the temple! "And He healed them" (v. 14).

We believe the word to the church today is this. When the Jesus of the Bible is clearly heard in the church, trivialities will be revealed, "tables" will be turned over, and religious pretenders will run for cover.

But in the end, the "blind" and "lame" will be strangely drawn and wonderfully healed by the grace of Jesus, who fights for them.

In college they called it "Rush Week." It was the time when the fraternities and sororities pulled out all the stops to recruit the most desirable new students into their house.

Jesus confronted false spiritual leaders for this very same thing. They went to great lengths to recruit people into a religion system, instead of to God. Have you ever felt like you were being recruited?

15

Spreading "the Gospel"

I was a freshman at Bethel College in Minnesota, (David speaking). It was a Sunday afternoon, and I was in my dorm room with some friends watching the Chicago Bears play the Minnesota Vikings. Being a die-hard Bears fan and going to school in the middle of "Vikingland" made this a game of significant interest. Halfway through the third quarter, three young men about my age came into the room. I'd never seen them before, and they quickly introduced themselves as being from a local Bible college with which I was familiar.

The situation began to feel awkward when they revealed that the reason they had come into our room was to "witness." They had come to "save" us. As I listened to their appeal, I decided not to react. *What they are doing is sincere*, I thought. *They have probably mistaken our Christian college for some evil secular university.* When they finished, I politely thanked them for coming, indicating that we had already received Christ as our Savior, loved Him with all our heart, and would serve Him forever—as soon as the game was over.

My attempt at humor did not amuse them. They made it clear in no uncertain terms that we could not possibly be among the redeemed for two obvious reasons:

1. We went to Bethel College.
2. We were watching a football game on Sunday—relaxing and enjoying ourselves, while lost men and women out there were on their way to hell. If we were Christians, we would be out witnessing every free moment.

At that point, I said something that convinced them that they were right about my unredeemed status. They left in a huff, probably convinced that they now knew how the prophets must have felt—being "persecuted for preaching the gospel."

But my temporary relief that they had gone was replaced quickly by a flood of unpleasant emotions. First, I felt angry and defensive, then intimidated and confused. I knew that you could only be saved by grace and that watching a football game on a Sunday afternoon would probably not cut me off from God's grace. But if this was true, why did I have the urge to run after them and convince them I was a legitimate Christian—to tell them about the people I had shared my faith with? Why this urgency to produce "proof" that I was really a believer?

In retrospect, I believe it was because of the load of guilt and shame these brothers laid on me. A load like that is one you immediately want to get rid of. One way would have been for me to convince them I was okay. I'd then have their blessing and the load would be gone—or some of it anyway. To get the "full blessing," I probably would have had to leave Bethel, get a very short haircut, and go to their school. (And, no more Bears games on Sunday afternoon!)

Ultimately, I count this as a good experience. It made me have to settle an important question: From whom, or from what, am I going to get my value, my sense of acceptability before God? Is it from my confidence in Jesus' finished work on the cross, or will it come from the opinion of others—even well-meaning Christians? I chose Jesus.

Telling "Good News"—or "Recruiting"?

Why did these three young men come to my room that day? Was it out of love? Excitement at the joy in their own lives? Was it a desire to lift the load of my shame and guilt with the message of God's amazing grace? It certainly did not feel as if they'd come to lift my load. Now I've come to see that they were there to lay their wearying load on me. In fact, I don't believe they were there to do something for *me* at all. They were doing it for themselves. They could not lose. If we rejected them, they were being persecuted for Christ. If we agreed with them, they had another "star in their crown."

Brothers and sisters in Christ, the time has come for us all to examine ourselves and what we mean by "spreading the good news" about Jesus Christ. Are we evangelizing—that is, spreading the heavenly message that begins, "Peace on earth, good will towards men"? Or are we recruiting? What kind of life are we recruiting people to? Are we seeking to liberate the burdened and lost—or, like these young men, are we still trying to validate ourselves? Paul warned those who were resorting to "spiritual performance" after having tasted grace that they were in grave danger of "boasting in your flesh" (Galatians 6:13).

Converted to Religion

The Pharisees with whom Jesus was contending in Matthew 23 were the ultimate examples of those who recruited people to a religious system and not to God. We already know, from Matthew 23:1–12, that they were *not* looking to lighten the load of distressed and downcast people. They were looking for people on whom they could lay a load of religious performance. The truth is they were not evangelizing, they were recruiting. They were not seeking to liberate the lost, they were seeking to validate themselves.

"Woe to you, scribes and Pharisees, hypocrites, because you travel about on sea and land to make one proselyte; and when he becomes one, you make him twice as much a son of hell as yourselves" (Matthew 23:15).

In the mind of a Pharisee there were two kinds of converts: the *proselyte of the gate*, and the *proselyte of righteousness*. Let's take a closer look at these two people to see whether or not we are in fact producing these types of converts with our "good news."

The Proselyte of the Gate

This person was a Gentile who, upon hearing of the One true God and the need to have faith in Him alone, believed in God. This person was what we would refer to today as a "simple believer." He doesn't know the right "language" or anything about a religious system, he just loves Jesus. This kind of convert was not very impressive to a Pharisee. The one who really counted was the next one.

The Proselyte of Righteousness

This was the person who, beyond loving God, "converted" to the system. He got circumcised, learned the rules, and embraced all the Levitical and traditional rituals. He became a Pharisee. This person might have begun with a heart hungry for God, but before he realized what was happening, knowing how to be a *good Pharisee* was more important than knowing how to be a *genuine man of God*.

How do we see this second scenario played out today? It can occur when people know more about what it means to be a Baptist, Catholic, Lutheran, Mennonite, Methodist, Evangelical, or Charismatic than what it means to be a simple, born-of-the-Spirit child of God. It occurs when people know more about their church tradition, denominational distinctives, governing bylaws, or church service preferences than they know about the Word of God. To the Pharisee, the one who went beyond simple love for God and converted to the system was the true convert.

"I'm of Paul, I'm of Apollos"

A friend named Jon reports that when he was a young child, he would watch Billy Graham crusades on television with his parents and grandmother. They would never miss one.

The adults cried, especially Grandma, when George Beverly Shea boomed out praises for God in his smooth, deep voice. There were verbal affirmations for the content of Dr. Graham's messages. There was always great delight when the scores of people would march down to the front. Then, almost as if on cue, an argument would break out between the adults and Dr. Graham—needless to say, a one-sided debate.

The argument began when, as the broadcast was coming to an end, Dr. Graham encouraged the new believers to find a church where they could worship God and grow as Christians.

"Why don't you send them to a Baptist church?" someone would pipe up angrily.

"What if they decide to go to a *Catholic* church?"

"There are a lot of wishy washy Lutherans out there. Why don't you tell them to worship with the Baptists?"

"Now I understand," says Jon, "why our celebration about the new converts always soured into a debate about denominations. It was more important to my family that people were *Baptist* than that they *loved Jesus.*"

This sounds similar to the issue Paul confronted in 1 Corinthians 3, where we can see the seeds of denominationalism. The Corinthians were saying, "I'm of Paul, I'm of Apollos, I'm of Cephas." Division and quarrels between members of the body of Christ were already happening, as these early Christians began to take their sense of value and identity from which pastor they followed. Paul confronts this mentality, saying: "I planted, Apollos watered, but God was causing the growth. So then neither the one who plants nor the one who waters is anything, but God who causes the growth" (vv. 6–7).

Christianity has always been about introducing people to Jesus Christ, the one true path to God; not about pet religious persuasions.

My Own Unhappy Surprise

I'd been a pastor of the church for less than six months (David speaking), so everything felt new, hopeful and possible. I regarded everyone there as a friend, and had no reason to think otherwise. Our denominational affiliation was the one aspect of the church with which I was still very unfamiliar. Theologically, I knew there were very few differences between the denomination I grew up in and the one I was now entering. But what about the inner workings? What about the heart? What did they care about? Was it progressive, or traditional? Was it open, or was it rigid? Was it graceful or was it legalistic?

From all I'd heard at the church, this denomination was the greatest thing going. Biblically sound, evangelistically zealous, and missions-minded. I was assured that I would "just love it." I left the office for my first denominational meeting with a sense of eager anticipation. It was a district meeting, a good place to get a feel for things. I would have my first chance to meet other pastors and find out what they cared about. I was eager to regard everyone as a friend.

On the fourth day of the conference, the president of the denomination's flagship college addressed the assembly. He had been newly installed as their youngest president ever. Enthusiasm was running high. I had particular interest in him simply because several years prior to my arrival he had been the youth pastor at the church I now pastored. I had never met him, but I'd heard all good things.

What he said in his address I will never forget. He started by lamenting the fact that a young girl who grew up under his ministry and went to our denomination's Bible college had married a man from another Bible college and entered ministry under the banner of another denomination. "We're losing our young people!" he warned. "We're raising them, we're training them, and then we're losing them." Losing them? He was talking about someone who had gone into full-time ministry with her husband—but it was not in *our* denomination, so we were "losing her."

To say I felt uneasy is an understatement. The college and seminary I attended certainly had flaws, but I had never heard this kind of talk. It had always been my understanding that the goal of a Bible college or seminary was to train people for ministry—period. Where that ministry was lived out seemed to be up to God. We were prepared and encouraged to go where we were called. It was, in fact, that perspective that allowed me to leave my original denomination and come to this one. The counsel I had received growing up was, "Listen to God. Do what He says. Go where He leads."

His comments might have been overlooked—if his address hadn't gotten worse. Not only did he lament the fact that people who grew up in this denomination were serving elsewhere, he began to expose the dangers of people who grew up elsewhere and were now serving "in here." His caution was to be careful about these people, because "they don't know our *distinctives*."

What were these distinctives? Were they different than Scripture? Were they *better* than Scripture? Were they *in* Scripture? What was going on here? I had checked out the doctrine, and this denomination was conservatively evangelical and to my estimation thoroughly biblical. If that was true, why couldn't someone come in from the outside and fit in? Why would they be a danger to the denomination?

I went past feeling uneasy. I tried to minimize it, to convince myself I hadn't heard clearly. He hadn't said it; he didn't mean it. But there was a problem. I had heard it, and others had "Amened" it.

I left that district meeting with the sickening sense that just loving Jesus would not be enough to fit in here. I would have to learn the rules, the traditions, the "distinctives." The message was clear: Being "this denomination" was more important than being filled with the Spirit, simple servants of the living God.

I wanted to run.

Conclusion

As we close this chapter, we would like to focus your thinking by asking several questions:

Does the "good news" you are hearing, or preaching, bring you to life and spiritual health, or does it not?

If the message you are hearing or preaching does not lift weights off people, set people free, and reconnect people to their true source of life—then is it the gospel?

If it is not the gospel, what will it do to its hearers?

We believe that the effects of trying to live under any message that is not the authentic "good news" from God will not be merely *neutral*. The effects will be *harmful*.

What will happen under such a message is that people will be harmed and harmed again. Even "devoured." This is a matter of grave importance, and a phenomenon we must now examine.

The marquee on the outside of the church building read, FIND LOVE INSIDE. Meanwhile the pastor was being indicted for becoming sexually involved with counselees. A dozen women, as well as their husbands and children, were devoured under the guise of getting healed.

In those religious systems where the sheep are there for the "needs" of the shepherd, people's lives get devoured.

16

The People Get Devoured

Woe to you, scribes and Pharisees, hypocrites, because you devour widows' houses, even while for a pretense you make long prayers; therefore you shall receive greater condemnation. (Matthew 23:14)

The picture of someone "devouring," while at the same time "offering long prayers," is both graphic and frightening. The appearance of spirituality gives birth to trust in the heart. We think, "This person really must love God. They must love me. This must be right." The result? A person responds to the *appearance*, rather than taking time to watch how their long-term relationship will unfold and whether or not it produces the fruit of trust, which is trustworthy actions.

The difficulty for so many people is that they have been trained in Scriptures and not in simple relationships. Or they are trained in only a certain segment of the Scriptures.

For instance, all through Scripture, we are given instructions to obey, follow and submit to spiritual leaders. Hebrews 13:17 states: "Obey your leaders, and submit to them; for they keep watch over your souls, as those who who give an account." In abusive systems, however, that verse is stripped of its spirit and translated legalistically to mean, "Don't think, don't discern, don't question, and don't notice problems." If you do, you will be labeled as unsubmissive, unspiritual, and divisive.

The fact of the matter is that while we should give "double honor" to those elders who "rule well" (1 Timothy 5:17), not all elders *rule well*. Spiritual leaders are people who prove over the long run that they know how to lead souls to peace. Jesus warned in Matthew 7:15 to beware of those "who come in sheep's clothing, but inwardly are ravenous wolves." We must remember that a wolf does not hate sheep—he just needs to consume them to satisfy his own hungers. It is the unsatisfied hungers—mentally, egotistically, emotionally—that cause a shepherd to devour his own. You follow, you trust, and you think it is completely safe.

A Childhood Devoured

Jill and her family attended a small church in the suburbs. She was a member of the youth group and involved in other activities. A church staff member had purchased a new car. Jill went for a ride in the new car with this trusted friend of the family. Once they were alone, however, he took sexual liberties with her. In the eyes of civil authorities, this would be called criminal sexual misconduct.

With a great deal of emotional difficulty and reluctance, Jill told her parents. They immediately told the church leadership, who assured Jill's parents that they would take care of the problem. The next thing the congregation knew, the staff member was gone—no explanation. There was no real *help* for Jill in the church, because she could not talk safely about her pain. Furthermore, rumors leaked. Before long, people blamed Jill—but since it is not Christian to talk about such things, each person only passed the rumor to his or her best friend (but of course everyone has a few best friends). Eventually, Jill and her family realized they were being avoided. Jill went into a spiritual and emotional tailspin. *She* was being shamed because the church leaders were covering a serious offense with silence.

Jill was abused by the staff member. Then she was "re-abused" by the leaders who covered up, saying, "Peace, peace," when there was no peace. She was re-abused by the people who blamed the victim. Because of the code of silence, it was impossible to know if there were other teenage victims who needed help as well. In addition, because the perpetrator wasn't held accountable for his actions, he went on to another church, only to victimize another teen. Because the abuse was covered up, those leaders of Jill's church share legal responsibility for the abuse that occurred in the other church. Are they also accountable before God for not acting when they had knowledge a crime was being committed? Yes!

Several years later, Jill met with the current elders of her church and her story broke their hearts. This time the elders *believed* her.

She shared the pain, confusion, and then betrayal she experienced as a result of the abuse and the way it was mishandled. She lost her self-esteem, her peer group, and the support of the church that had been a vital part of her life up to that point. That was a deep enough grief. Her emotions were so shattered she was afraid to ride in a car with her own dad, one of the most laid-back, gentle men you'd ever want to meet. Before the abuse she'd had normal friendships. After the abuse and all the confusion, inappropriate sexual relationships seemed right. And now, right sex seems wrong.

In our thinking, Jill's childhood and thirteen years since were devoured. She was victimized on Saturday by a person with leadership on Sunday. Instead of using his authority and influence to build and strengthen, he misused it in a perverse attempt to meet his own needs. Thirteen years later, she is still reaping the emotional fruit of the way the church devoured a wounded girl.

On the night the elders met with Jill, the Lord began to restore to her what had been taken. She will be seeking counseling. And after thirteen years, she was believed by spiritual leaders, who grieve with her.[1]

The person who committed the abuse was neglected and wounded as well. Instead of receiving help, healing and accountability, he was discarded or ignored. Many more years were devoured because help was not offered! But God is good, and after all these years, the one who committed the abuse has also entered a recovery process and is experiencing God's grace and healing.

And Jill's family was devoured as well. Feel her mother's pain as you read this letter she wrote five years after Jill's abuse:

My daughter was molested by a church staff member when she was 13 years old. My husband wanted to confront him regarding his behavior. My husband and I went to an elder to get direction, assistance and support. We wanted him to go with us to confront the staff member. But the elder, my husband, and I did not confront the church staff member. The elder and his wife became involved. The elder, his wife and his children became involved. The elder, his wife, his children, and fellow elders became involved. The elder, his wife, his children, fellow elders, and their families became involved. The elder, his wife, his children, fellow elders, their families and the church became

---

[1] Jill wants the readers to know that this edited version of her story can only begin to touch on the true-life pain and confusion which, with God's help, she believes she will overcome.

involved. They discussed, diagnosed and analyzed our pain.

*Our pain became gossip. We were never counseled or sup-
ported. Our pain increased. People came to me. One said, "Well,
your daughter was 'that way.' " Another said, "It had to be the
way she dressed." Another said, "She asked for it." We nearly
broke under the pain.*

God help me!

*It hurts so bad. My daughter is in pain. My God, won't some-
one love my daughter, my children? Can they not see how dev-
astated we are? Can they not know? Do they not understand?
It was not her fault. How could someone actually go up to her
and tell her it was her fault? . . . Can they not see? I am in pain,
she is in pain. She is confused, I am confused . . . And the church
goes on.*

*He violated her person. He took away her self-esteem. He
made her feel dirty and ugly and humiliated and worthless as
a human being . . . And more pain goes on.*

*They fired him, and then she was told it was her fault that
he got fired. I was told it was her fault that he got fired. But she
did it by being honest and open . . . And the church goes on.*

*I stood by and watched. I watched as she tried to "live above
the situation." I tried to encourage. I watched as she kept striving
to be accepted as a human being, in pain. I watched as the
discussing and analyzing and diagnosing went on and on. I
watched as the gossip totally enveloped a teenager's life. I
watched as my daughter gradually began to believe that she
was to blame. I watched as she tried to deal with the incredible
amount of pain by trying to take her own life. I watched as her
sibling became confused. I watched as her sibling began being
rejected. I watched as my children were both rejected and rejected and rejected and . . . God, help me. Help them. Help the
church. God take this pain. . . .*

*I reached out to you and tried talking about my pain, the
situation. One said, "I don't want to talk about it. I don't want
to become involved." Another said, "You need to forgive and
forget. You have an unforgiving spirit." Still another said, "You
didn't spend enough time with her. If you had this never would
have happened."*

*But I don't understand, Lord. The pain is so overwhelm-
ing . . . Does anyone out there hear me?*

*Five years later she continues suffering the rejection of the
church. Her sibling has now experienced the rejection, the gossip, the exploitation, the pain. We have spent $3,000 on coun-
seling and medical expenses directly related to that painful*

experience and the process of rejection and unresolved pain.
She has now accepted "the fact" that the church thinks she's
bad, and that she is to blame.
And the pain goes on, and the church goes on . . .[2]

Role Reversal

You may say that this is an extreme case—and it is. But let's look at how people are devoured in more subtle forms, through what we refer to as "role reversal."

Role reversal is simply the dynamic that occurs when, instead of the leaders being there for the true well-being of the flock, the flock is there for the well-being of the leaders. Instead of the leaders using their strength, authority and knowledge to build, protect and nurture, they use those qualities to insure their own power, control, or recognition.

Several Scripture passages, in both the Old and New Testaments, reveal that this is not a new problem. (See Ezekiel 34; Zechariah 11; 2 Peter 2.) Abusive systems don't serve and equip people, they use people. Worse, they use people up.

"Devouring" Happens in Many Ways

While most Christian leaders would want desperately to distance themselves from believing that they devour people, we are more inclined to it than we know. Damaging consequences often come in very subtle packages.

For example, who among us doesn't struggle from time to time with getting our sense of value from what we do or how we look? What makes this spiritually dangerous is that many of us have had it deeply ingrained that what makes us "okay" is how well we perform whatever the prescribed "spiritual" behavior happens to be, and demand that others do the same.

Let's say the focus of our hope for value is a position in the church. Rather than pointing to Jesus, what is really valued is how well we perform in church. Eventually, we realize that memorizing and spouting Scripture, witnessing and leading study groups are terribly inadequate sources of life, in and of themselves, leaving us empty and looking for more.

How many of us thought, "I know, I'll go into the ministry. Nothing

---

[2]This story and this letter are used with permission.

could be more rewarding or fulfilling than that." Of course, good motives can and usually are entwined with false motives. And tangled together, perhaps, with a true desire to serve God is also the need to fill the sense of emptiness and worthlessness deep in our spirit. God would certainly approve, and so would the Christian community.

So let's say here I am: A new Christian leader, with lots of drive, lots of ambition, a Bible in my briefcase and a mission in my heart. The mission? To build the church! To advance the kingdom! These are wonderful sentiments to be sure; but part of "working out my own salvation with fear and trembling" will be to remember that there is a significant problem lurking in the shadows of my soul. The problem is subtle, and very dangerous. It is this: Unless I stay rightly connected to God, my entire sense of value as a person will come from how I perform as a person and how others reward and applaud my behavior. When we cross this inner line, something wrong begins to take place. I may encourage you to come and serve and give to the glory of God, but the real reason I'm encouraging you to do that is because I will look like a success if you do. I will use you to make me look good. At this point, my ego has begun to feed upon you.

One church newsletter contained the following appeal from the pastor to attend church more regularly:

> Let me give you an inside look at what goes on in the pastor's mind when he notices that you aren't coming to all of the services provided by the church (Sunday Morning, Sunday Evening, Sunday School, Wednesday Prayer Meeting, and Saturday Men's Breakfasts.)
>
> 1. He must be really sick. (He'll be back when he's better.)
> 2. Perhaps he got called in to work. (He'd be here if he could.)
> 3. Maybe he's out of town. (Just a temporary absence.)
> 4. He's upset with me about something. (Uh-oh!)
> 5. He thinks I'm a terrible preacher. (How many others think that, too?)
> 6. He's looking for a different church to attend. (Gulp!)
> 7. He's in his backyard burning his hymnal and Sunday School lesson outlines. (I'm a total failure as a pastor.)

Think about this. In this pastor's mind, what is the reason for people to come to church? To find God? Life? Worship? No. It is to make sure their pastor does not feel like a total failure. The real issue here is that if nobody comes, or gives, or serves, he will look bad. If he gets his value from how he performs, he *can't* let that happen!

Therefore, he will pressure, plead and manipulate so that you will come.

Little Sheep Get "Devoured" Too

Recently I had a counseling appointment with Sally, the daughter of a minister (Jeff speaking). She told how she would avoid the pastoral staff of our church on Sundays, and would stay away from them in the fellowship center between services. If one of the ministers was standing in a doorway, she would go way out of her way to go through another door. It took all of her courage to even see me, another minister.

During the first few tense minutes of our session, she told how much a certain sermon that Dave Johnson preached had meant to her. I said, "Oh, that's great. You ought to tell him sometime."

Sally turned ashen gray, and literally lost her breath.

Where did such a deep fear come from? Here is a bit of Sally's story.

When Sally was little, she would sometimes get colds and the flu, like normal little children do. During those times when she was suffering from these normal childhood afflictions, she was isolated from the rest of her family—especially from her dad, the minister. Why? Because he had to preach to his flock, and he could not afford for his people to see him sick and weak—and he had to be there "for them." What would happen to his church if he missed preaching one Sunday? So his little girl sat in her room, isolated and sick, because God "needed" her dad so badly, when really it was the little girl who needed her dad.

The "need" to look good grew more intense.

Once, when Sally was acting in front of some church people in a way that was embarrassing to her parents, her father took her by the arm. With a smile on his face, he dug his fingers into her under the armpit, scolding her under his breath.

Later on that day, Sally's arm began to swell. Then it started to throb; then it went numb. Finally, with her arm almost twice its normal size, she was taken to the emergency room. Her dad had injured a blood vessel, cutting off the circulation in her arm.

As appalling as the injury itself was the incident that happened afterwards. Instead of taking her to the local hospital, Sally's parents drove to the hospital in a neighboring town—they didn't want to run into anyone they knew. When they arrived, they didn't rush their daughter into the emergency room, but instead, all three of them waited in the car in the parking lot, hoping that the swelling would go down by itself. That way they could avoid accountability and possible confrontation altogether.

There was never an apology. In fact, Sally was treated as though she were to blame. Her mom justified the dad's behavior to Sally: "How does it look when the minister's daughter acts that way? What will people say about your father?"

Through the course of subsequent sessions with Sally, I listened to example after example of how she had to live to protect the self-esteem of her father, "the mighty man of God." It took her years before she could knowingly sit in the same room with a pastor.

Sally, like so many today, was used up so that a very human man would not have to admit his imperfections, but could instead show the world he was a "good minister."

As Paul once said to the Corinthian church, "Brothers and sisters, these things should not be!"

Conclusion

The characteristics of abuse dealt with thus far wound and devour people. Now it is time to move on to Part 3, where we will examine the steps needed to bring healing from spiritual abuse.

Part III

Post-Abuse Recovery

Introduction to Part III

Recovery

By now we've made our position clear. Spiritual abuse is a problem we believe to be widespread and also deeply ingrained in our contemporary Christian culture. On a personal level, it harms or overloads people who need spiritual weight lifted off them. And in terms of the "gospel message," it presents a wrong message about the life of grace and faith—one that ultimately leads to no life at all.

We've also presented an extended portrait of the way Jesus confronted the perpetrators of spiritual abuse in His day, with an offer of healing and rest to all who would cease their religious labors and turn to Him.

Unfortunately, we realize that many spiritual leaders and systems are so ingrained in their thinking that an invitation to rest in the finished work of Christ will seem "impossible," "unrealistic," or even "unscriptural." And so we turn, in this section, to an offer of counsel and hope for those who have been victimized by any form of spiritual abuse. Our interest is to offer steps of healing and recovery. We will also offer guidance that may help you in determining whether or not a spiritually abusive system can be changed, and whether or not God's plan for you includes staying within a system to change it (*fight*), or to leave for a safer spiritual climate (*flight*).

Ultimately, of course, our aim is to guide you back into a stronger, healthier relationship with God.

"Why does this keep happening to me?" This is a question frequently asked by people coming out of spiritually abusive religious systems. For some, it is because spiritually abusive systems are actually spiritual "traps" that fit with the wounds people have experienced in other unhealthy relationships. Understanding this dynamic can help you leave the abusive system and prevent you from falling into another trap in the future.

17

How to Escape a Spiritual Trap

When I was a kid (Jeff speaking), my family would spend the summers at a beautiful, private lake. In order to be able to fish as much as we wanted to, my brother and I would catch our own minnows for bait.

The most effective method was to use a minnow trap like the one illustrated here. We would put crackers inside for bait and lower the trap from the end of the dock until it rested on the bottom of the lake. Minnows would swim by the opening and see the bait inside. Once they swam in through the opening, however, they could not find their way back out of the hole. It was a great trap.

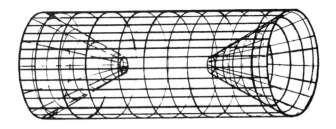

"Good" Traps

Several elements need to be present, however, for any trap to work, including the trap of a spiritually abusive system.[1] First, a good trap makes it easy for the prey to get in, but hard to get out.

---

[1]Jeffrey Z. Rubin, "Psychological Traps." *Psychology Today* (March 1981).

If it didn't have this quality, it would not be a trap. (This is why fish hooks have barbs, for instance.) Second, there needs to be attractive bait. Really good bait will occupy the attention of the prey so thoroughly that the danger will go unnoticed. Third, once in the trap, the more the prey struggles, the more tired and trapped it becomes. Wolf traps have teeth, and the more a wolf struggles, the deeper the teeth bite. The more it hurts, the harder the wolf struggles, and the vicious cycle keeps repeating until the wolf has struggled to death.

Finally, a trap has to "fit" with the prey it is being used to catch. You can't catch minnows with a wolf trap, or wolves with a minnow trap. Not only this, but the more you know about the prey, the more effective trap you can devise.

Let's see how all this applies. Ultimately, the more we know about a trap, the clearer will be our understanding of how to escape and begin healing.

Spiritual Traps

In a very real sense, the spiritually abusive system is a spiritual trap. And not just any old trap; a "good" one.

As we've already seen, spiritually abusive systems are easy to get into but hard to leave. The leaders assume power and demand obedience. They foster loyalty to the organization with implied or overt scare tactics and threats. Leaving the system is equal to leaving God and His protection. Paranoia about the evils outside the system makes people afraid to leave. This begins the building of a trap. Then comes the *bait*.

There are many kinds of bait in the spiritually abusive church, family or organization. "Right standing with God" is probably the most common bait. In 2 Corinthians 11:13–15, Paul says that false apostles "disguise themselves as servants of righteousness." The abusive system gives people an opportunity to earn God's approval with their own positive self-effort. In fact, this bait is so appealing that people fail to notice several things.

For instance, they learn to ignore others around them who point out that they are being neglected or mistreated. They overlook it when they grow more tired as time goes on. They ignore the fact that people close to them are leaving and urging them to leave. They are oblivious to how it is becoming easier to justify the things that not too long ago they abhorred.

Other baits might include: the approval of people; religious status or position; a paycheck; the promise that things will improve; or an opportunity to be shamed and mistreated in a way that is consistent with their sense of deserving to be punished for being so "bad."

In addition to everything else these people ignore, they overlook the fact that their goal keeps moving out of reach. This reveals the third aspect of a good trap. Like the donkey who runs faster to reach the "carrot on a stick," the bait draws people deeper and deeper into the abusive religious system. (At least the minnows get the crackers.) If they want to stop struggling, a voice within "warns" them: "What if you give up now, just when you were about to have a spiritual 'breakthrough'?" So they cannot stop.

This introduces the concept of *equity rescuing*. When people do this with a house, we call the house a "money pit." Money pits are houses that suck people's money into an endless home-improvement mission. This happens because they invest money into the house to make it more livable. But more things keep going bad. Then more money is needed to continue the improvements. After a while, more and more investment is needed to "rescue" all the money already put into the house. This also happens with jobs. After ten years in a job you hate, your conversation with yourself goes something like this: "I hate this job. I think I'll quit. Wait a minute, I can't quit. If I quit I'll have wasted the past ten years. I'll stay for another year. If things don't improve in a year, then I'll quit." The problem is that in a year you have another year's "equity" to rescue. And you'd have to walk away from eleven years instead of ten, so it's harder to leave than before.

"Equity rescuing" occurs in abusive relationships, as well. Look at the following illustration. The point on the left represents healthy and normal. In an abusive situation people are mistreated: physically, sexually, emotionally, or spiritually. This represents a movement away from normal.

The next abuse represents another movement away from normal. Likewise, the next, and the next.

You end up far away from normal. You may even be well aware that the situation is abusive and abnormal. So you set up a "boundary." You say, "What's happened up until now is *it*. No more! I'll stay, but if this happens one more time, I'm leaving." It happens again, but for you to walk away from the situation at this point will feel as if you have been abused for nothing. So you try a little bit harder, and invest a little more of yourself. More serious abuse occurs, so you set up another boundary. "You can call me names and push me around, but if I ever get a scar or a black eye, *then* I quit." Soon the abuser gives you that black eye, which moves the situation still farther away from healthy and normal.

The problem is that most victims assess their present situation only by comparing it to the last adjustment. Compared to all they have invested, this latest violation just isn't that big of a compromise.

They don't compare it to *normal*. If a victim does compare their situation to *normal*, they would be able to see how many unhealthy adjustments they have made and how really abnormal and unhealthy the relationship has become.

It's ironic that the fact that we care so much about our faith is what contributes to our being trapped in unhealthy systems. We care about the kingdom of God. We care about real things, about things that last forever. We want to invest in that. We want to put our energy, our time, and our money there. Shouldn't the church be the best investment? But things go sour, and sometimes our efforts turn into an equity-rescuing venture. It is hard to walk away from relationships, even if they are hurtful or abusive. It would be like losing all of our relational equity.

How We "Fall Prey"

As we noted earlier, the final aspect of a good trap is that it is well-suited to the prey it is designed to catch. This can certainly be said of spiritually abusive systems. The "harmony" or "fit" between the characteristics of spiritually abusive systems and the characteristics of victims is uncanny.

In order to illustrate this, we will list each of the characteristics of the spiritually abusive system as presented earlier. Next to each one we will place the effects that shame-based relationships have on people, those characteristics that contribute to the *learned powerlessness* we discussed earlier in Chapter Four. Notice the fit.

Characteristics of the Spiritually Abusive System (THE TRAP)	Learned Powerlessness: Effects of Previous Shame-Based Relationships on Victims (THE PREY)
1. Power Posturing	Distorted image of God; high level of anxiety based on other people or external circumstances; people-pleasing; a high need to be punished or to pay for mistakes in order to feel okay; ignore your "radar" because you're being "too critical"; high need for structure; difficulty saying "no"; allowing others to take advantage of you.

2. Performance-Preoccupation	Perfectionism, or giving up without trying; doing only those things that you're good at; lack of self-discipline; can't make or admit mistakes; procrastination; view of God as more concerned with how you act than who you are; can't rest when tired; can't have guilt-free fun; high need for the approval of others; sense of shame or self-righteousness; demanding of others; you're hard on your kids, or you don't expect enough from them; negative view of self, even self-hate; negative self-talk; shaming others; defensive "skills" (blaming, rationalizing, minimizing, lying); difficulty forgiving self; difficulty accepting grace and forgiveness from God; feeling selfish for having needs; rescuing others from the consequences of their behaviors.
3. Unspoken Rules	Great "radar," or the ability to pick up tension in situations and relationships; ability to decode the crooked messages of others; saying things in code instead of saying them straight; talking about people instead of to them; expecting others to know your code; reading other meanings into what people say.
4. Lack of Balance	High need to control thoughts, feelings and behaviors of others; out-of-touch with feelings, needs, thoughts; guess at what is normal; stress-related illness; continually letting unsafe people come close; extreme forms of denial, even delusion.
5. Paranoia	The sense that if something is wrong or someone is upset you must have caused it; a sense that if there is a problem, you have to solve it; feel like no one else understands you; threatened by opinions that differ from yours; afraid to take healthy risks; suspicious or afraid of others; putting up boundaries that keep safe people away; feelings of guilt when you haven't done anything wrong; difficulty trusting people.
6. Misplaced Loyalty	Need to be right; critical of others; giving others the "third degree"; narrow-minded; fear of being deserted; possessive in relationships.
7. Code of Silence	Self-analytical; rebelling against structure; feeling alone; living a double life; message-carrying for people; can't ask for help.

Delusion

In 2 Corinthians 11, Paul warned Christians, "But I am afraid, lest as the serpent deceived Eve by his craftiness, your *minds* should be *led astray* from the simplicity and purity of devotion to Christ" (v. 3). In a very real sense, people trapped in spiritually abusive systems have had their minds led astray. It seems that at some point, they cross a line in their ability to see what is happening to them. Let's now describe that line, because it is the inner boundary that will need to be rebuilt as escape and recovery begin.

If you recall, we have described denial as the God-given ability to avoid feeling emotional, psychological or spiritual pain. When the amount of pain associated with a situation is too much to bear, we numb-out emotionally. It's a gift to help us enter the process that will help us eventually accept and deal with the situation. However, there are unhealthy ways a person might intentionally deny the existence of a situation, including: lying, blaming others, minimizing the seriousness, rationalizing, or ignoring. This form of denial is more serious. It is "exchanging the truth for a lie," which results in a "depraved mind" (Romans 1:25, 28). At that point, the mind can no longer tell the difference between what is true and what is false.

This phenomenon is called *delusion* and it is the end result of conscious forms of denial. Delusion is the distorted perception of reality, a totally unrealistic view of what is real. Conscious denial has to exist in a spiritual abuse situation in order to convince others that everything is fine, and also to fix blame away from the person or system. When it succeeds in convincing the person himself or herself, *he or she is deluded.*

Delusion is one of the main components in the learned powerlessness of the victim. More serious than denial, different than repression, it is a warp in the thinking process that filters out or twists information coming in from the outside. It is probably the most significant factor in keeping the victim trapped in the abusive system.

Religious Addiction

Chemical dependency is the state of being dependent on a mood-altering substance. It is the end result of depending on a "false god" more and more to meet needs it is not capable of meeting. Time, energy, honesty, money and relationships with others are invested and lost in the addiction process. And more investments are needed to rescue past investments. As denial turns to delusion, addicts loose sight of how the chemical is hurting them and how their own life is affecting others. Friends offer warnings, but to no avail. They are mastered by chemicals.[2]

In spiritually abusive systems you can mood-alter as well. You can employ your unhealthy relationship skills "for God," rather than taking the painful course of receiving help to change them. You can rescue people from the consequences of their behaviors and be a hero. You can exercise personal power and opinions and call it God. Working to earn the approval of God and others is *spiritual mood-altering*. The state of being dependent on a spiritually mood-altering system is called "religious addiction."

You invest more and more of your life in a system that promises but cannot deliver. More investments are required to justify past investments. You deny what you see, how you feel, how tired you are, and the problems you have, and call it spiritual. As denial turns to delusion you lose sight of how the system has actually begun to hurt you and how your own life is hurting others. Your friends try to warn you, but you cannot hear. You are caught in the trap of the spiritually abusive system.

In their book, *Toxic Faith*, Stephen Arterburn and Jack Felton offer the following test as a tool in order to discern religious addiction.[3] How would you answer their questions?

1. *Has your family complained that you are always going to a church meeting, rather than spending time with them?*
2. *Do you feel extreme guilt for being out of church just one Sunday?*
3. *Do you sense that God is looking at what you do, and if you don't do enough He might turn on you or not bless you?*
4. *Are you giving money to a ministry because you believe God will make you wealthy if you give?*
5. *Have you ever been involved with a minister sexually?*
6. *Is it hard for you to make decisions without consulting your minister? Even small ones?*
7. *Do you ever have thoughts of God wanting you to destroy yourself or others in order to go and live with Him?*
8. *Do you believe you are still being punished for something you did as a child?*

---

[2]Jeff VanVonderen, *Good News for the Chemically Dependent and Those Who Love Them* (Nashville, Tenn.: Thomas Nelson, 1991).
[3]Stephen Arterburn and Jack Felton, *Toxic Faith* (Nashville, Tenn.: Oliver-Nelson Publishers, 1991).

9. *Do you feel if you work a little harder, God will finally forgive you?*
10. *Has anyone ever told you a minister was manipulating your thoughts or feelings?*

Conclusion

The reason people stay in spiritually abusive systems is that somehow they "fit" so well. In order to break free, several things need to happen.

First, victims have to reach the point where they realize they are being spiritually abused, and ask for help. They must be given the information and permission necessary to call what they've experienced "abuse."

Second, they need a renewal of the mind. In a very real sense they've been spiritually brainwashed. They must be immersed in the truth about who God really is and what He has lovingly done to settle the issue of their value and acceptance. They need to hear the good news about their new *gift-based* identity.

Third, they must experience safe relationships in which to heal from their emotional, psychological and spiritual wounds. Admitting neediness is hard. Looking at yourself honestly and fearlessly is hard. Much support is needed.

Fourth—again, in the context of safe relationships—they must be given permission and opportunities to practice getting their sense of identity as a gift from Jesus.

In the next chapter, we will focus on the process of renewing the mind.

In truth, who people are is not really determined by what others have done to them. Each of us interpret the meaning of our experiences and make decisions in response. In supportive relationships where correct interpretations and decisions can be made, even extremely wounding circumstances can turn out for health.

In spiritually abusive systems, however, wounds are added to wounds. Lies are believed and defenses strengthened. In order to recover from spiritual abuse, people need to hear the truth. They need to understand the choices. They need a renewal of the mind.

18

Renewing the Mind

Molly was a client of mine (Jeff speaking) who had a constant struggle with accepting God's grace.

"Why do you think it hard for you to remember that God loves you and His stance toward you is 'yes'?" I asked.

"That's easy," she replied, with barely a moment's deliberation. "Because I know myself so well. I know all my shortcomings, and I know how far I still have to go."

God's stance toward us is "earned" and settled by Jesus. Yet how many of us have been trained to "put to death the deeds of the flesh" by becoming preoccupied with *self* and with "spiritual behaviors"? We have forgotten that preoccupation with self in the name of God is still preoccupation with self. But after all, if righteousness and holiness are up to me, I had better pay very close attention to myself.

Even though Molly is no longer in an abusive system, she continues to revert back to measuring herself by herself. The good news is, there is a way to recover.

It's "Lawman"!

We would like to invent a video game for Christians called "Lawman." Various buildings and locations on the screen would represent places where a person can get support to help them live the Christian life. A colored bar on the bottom of the screen would represent the player's spiritual energy level. As the player, your job is to go around the screen living the Christian life. You pray for a mom who has cancer, asking God to give her a gift of healing and inner comfort. You tell a burned-out workaholic that life and rest is in Jesus and His work on the cross. You give food to some folks that need it. Sometimes, you say no to everyone who wants your time, in order to say yes to your family. Once in a while you even have to pray against demonic activity. Sometimes you rest and do nothing. Or you just think about God's grace, and you are amazed to be His beloved son or daughter.

On your journey, however, you will receive numerous messages about how defective you are, that you are not doing enough. You get wounded or tired. Or you forget who you are, and to Whom you belong. People's opinions become more important. You begin keeping track of your religious behavior. You start trying to earn what is yours for free. You need some good news!

So you pick up a Christian book from a well-meaning friend. Or you enter the home of another Christian for a Bible study, or a local hotel where a Christian seminar is taking place. You may even go into a church building. These places look safe.

But do these "safe" places really offer opportunities to simply bask in God's love and grace? Where is the good news that His approval is a gift, earned and settled on the basis of what Jesus did and not based on what you do? Where are the reminders that your identity in Christ is established and sealed by the Holy Spirit? And where are the hugs for your sadness, the tears for your wounds, or the rest for your tiredness?

You begin to pick up other signals. You've felt this way before. Your spiritual energy bar takes a sudden dip. Your spiritual alarm goes off . . . It's "Lawman"! He marches out, swinging the Bible—Wocka! Wocka! Wocka!—and begins to give you various spiritual jobs to do. With each job, your energy bar gets shorter. Your energy drops and drops.

"Where then is that sense of blessing you once had?" Paul asks in Galatians 4:15. "It was for freedom that Christ set us free; therefore keep standing firm and do not be subject again to a yoke of slavery. You were running well; who hindered you from obeying the truth? This persuasion did not come from Him who calls you" (Galatians 5:1, 7–8).

No Test

There is no test to diagnose spiritual abuse. There are only spiritual clues: lack of joy in the Christian life; tiredness from trying hard to measure up; disillusionment about God and spiritual things; uneasiness, lack of trust, or even fear of those who care about "God" things, even legitimately; a profound sense of missing your best Friend; cynicism or grief over good news that turned out to be too good to be true.

How can these things be? Jesus claimed to have come to bring rest and abundant life. David said, in Psalm 86:5:

For Thou, Lord, are good, and ready to forgive, and abundant in lovingkindness to all who call upon Thee.

And Paul said, in Romans 5:17:

. . . [how] much more those who receive the abundance of grace and of the gift of righteousness will reign in life through the One, Jesus Christ.

And in Philippians 4:19, he says:

And my God shall supply all your needs according to His riches in glory in Christ Jesus.

In 1 Peter 2:9–10, Peter said:

But you are a chosen race, a royal priesthood, a holy nation, a people for God's own possession, that you may proclaim the excellencies of Him who has called you out of darkness into His marvelous light; for you once were not a people, but now you are the people of God; you had not received mercy, but now you have received mercy.

You love God, and at one time you experienced His fullness. Why is this no longer your experience?

In Romans 12:2 Paul says, "And do not be conformed to this world, but be transformed by the renewing of your mind." This means, do not be squeezed from the outside in, but be changed from the inside out. The Greek word for "transform" means to be changed the way a caterpillar turns into a butterfly. It means something that is done *to* you, not *by* you. Paul is not saying, "Change yourself." He is saying that by a renewing of the mind you *will be* changed.

In Colossians 3, Paul says, "Set your mind on the things above, not on the things that are on earth" (v. 2). Let us consider how we have learned to set our minds on the things that are on earth.

A Problem from the Beginning . . .

In Psalm 51:5–6 David says, "Behold, I was brought forth in iniquity, and in sin my mother conceived me."

David is not trying to tell us, as some would say, that sex is evil.

Neither is he saying that his mother was sinning when she conceived him. These verses fall within the context of a prayer—contrite sinner to gracious God—for God to change his *condition*. David was aware that his condition fell short from "day one." From his very beginning he was in need of finding a way to hit the mark with God. As you will see in a moment, he found a way.

Likewise, we are born as needy beings into a world that promises to meet those needs. What the world offers, however, is not capable of doing so. We devise strategies in an attempt to meet our own needs. But with each and every one, we sin—we *miss the mark*, which is the prominent definition of sin in the New Testament. This is true whether our efforts are positive or negative. We may become capable at many endeavors, surround ourselves with many things, and acquire for ourselves the approval of many. But from "day one" we need a new identity, not just new behaviors. And we are incapable of doing anything to accomplish that. In Romans 5:6, Paul refers to this as our "helpless" condition.

. . . And All Along the Way

As we grew, each of us experienced relationships that sent us shaming messages. In doing so they have defined our identity as bad and defective, and then equipped us with faulty skills to remedy our defectiveness. Let us illustrate how this happens.

Beth, who was now 30, was the youngest of five children, with two older brothers and two older sisters. She had always sensed that somehow she didn't quite "fit" in her family. She couldn't put her finger on anything that was ever said. Nevertheless, she felt unwanted and her relationship with her mother always felt strained. Not long ago the two of them were spending an afternoon together when, out of curiosity, Beth asked her mom, "How many kids did you and Daddy want?" "Four," came the response. She was cut to the heart. Later on that day, they were in a restaurant when one of her mom's newest friends came up to say hello. "Who's this?" the woman asked, referring to Beth.

Her mom replied, "This is my youngest daughter."

"How many children do you have?" inquired the friend.

Through tears, Beth later shared with me her mother's answer, a response that suddenly made sense of what she had felt growing up: "Mom told this woman, 'We have two sons, two daughters, and *another* daughter.'"

Shame on You!

Each of us is surrounded by external sources of shame. These vary, of course. Families where people are called names or compared, or where parents have their needs met by the performance of the children, instill messages of shame in their members. Sexual, physical and, emotional abuse send shaming messages. Billboards, magazine ads and television commercials shame us by promising that some product has the power to make us more powerful, valuable, lovable or capable—thus reinforcing the mindset that in our present condition we are defective. Spiritually abusive relationships demand performance and shame us for not measuring up.

The message of condemnation is not limited to our actions or appearance. It is directed toward and lands on *us*: "You are the problem." "You are in the way." "Big boys don't cry." "Isn't that just like a girl." "You are stupid, fat, ugly, incompetent, lazy, worthless, selfish." "Shame on *you!*" This attacks the very core of our identity.

The Incorrect Response

Outside of a relationship with Jesus Christ, the Giver of Life, people lack life. Not only are our actions defective, *we* are defective. This is not to say that God does not love us. He loves us very much! Psalm 117 says:

Praise the Lord, all nations; laud Him, all peoples! For His lovingkindness is great toward us [all], and the truth of the Lord is everlasting.

In Matthew 5:45, Jesus says:

He [the Father] causes His sun to rise on the evil and the good, and sends rain on the righteous and the unrighteous.

For God so loved the world!

The fact that we are defective simply means that our problem is who we are—dead, helpless sinners, defective in our ability to fix our condition. Trying hard to change behaviors in order to have a positive self-concept is absolutely the wrong response. At best, it leads to more shame if we fail, or to self-righteousness if we succeed. At worst, it gives people who lack life the illusion of having life, and that we have earned God's approval.

Romans 10:11 reinforces: "For the Scripture says, 'Whoever believes in Him will not be put to shame.' " What this means, for those of us who have a relationship with Christ, is that *trying hard to change behaviors in order to correct a negative self-concept is the wrong response*. It results from not understanding or believing that our sin and shame are completely erased and our new identity has already been created by the activity of God. It erodes the Christian life into the tired state of self-effort aimed at fixing a negative self—a self that God has already replaced with a new creation! What a sad waste of time.

A Twist

There are some people who, rather than trying to do good behaviors to fix their shame, actually learn to act in ways that are consistent with their shame.

Take the case of a husband who beats his wife (bad behavior). What does the behavior say to this man about his condition? "You are a bad, defective husband!" How should this man feel about being so defective? Shamed and bad, of course. What is the best way for this husband to feel as shamed, bad and defective as he *should* feel for beating his wife? Keep beating his wife.

What about a person who overeats (unhealthy behavior)? What does this behavior say? "You are a weak, fat, unspiritual, undisciplined person!" How should they feel for being such a weak, fat, unspiritual person who overeats? Bad, defective, shamed. What is the best way for them to feel as bad, defective, and shamed as they should for being such a weak, fat person who overeats? Continue to overeat.

Now let's translate this into "spiritual" behaviors. Let's say a person does not read the Bible. What does that say about them? "You are a bad, unspiritual Christian!" How should they feel for being such a bad, unspiritual Christian who doesn't read the Bible? Bad, defective, and shamed. What's the best way for them to feel as bad, defective and shamed as they should feel for being such a bad, unspiritual Christian who doesn't read the Bible? Continue to avoid reading the Bible.

What is the answer to our dilemma? It is neither to *try harder*, nor to *give up*. It begins as our mind is renewed and grows accustomed to the fact that we are a new creation.

In Galatians 6, Paul says, "For neither is circumcision anything, nor uncircumcision, but a new creation" (v. 15). As you can see, the focus of the struggle we have described so far is exactly opposite of Paul's focus. We struggle in vain to change external behaviors and situations, not *identity*. And, as we've seen, the harder we work to control behaviors, the more convinced we become that the answer for everyone else is to work hard, too.

Setting Our Minds on the Things Above

Each of us has been programmed to look outside of ourselves for the definition of our identity. The behaviors and opinions of others, our own behaviors, the things we collect—all these responses have told us who we are. In Philippians 3, Paul calls this "a mind to put confidence in the flesh."

It is at this point we must look again at Psalm 51. David, having begun at the right place spiritually—broken, poor in spirit—immediately lifts his eyes to the right source of life. He immediately asks God to intervene on his behalf. He's not simply asking to be "fixed up," but to be re-created: "Create in me a clean heart . . . Purify me, and I shall be clean."

Describing what God promises He *will* do, the prophet Ezekiel says, in chapter 36, "Then I will sprinkle clean water on you, and you will be clean; I will cleanse you from all your filthiness and from all your idols. Moreover, *I will give you a new heart and put a new spirit within you*" (vv. 25–26).

It is truly a wonder, all that God has done for us. Hebrews 10:22 says:

Let us draw near with a sincere heart in full assurance of faith, having our hearts sprinkled clean from an evil conscience and our bodies washed with pure water.

In Titus 3:5–6 Paul says:

He saved us, not on the basis of deeds which we have done in righteousness, but according to His mercy, by the washing of regeneration and renewing by the Holy Spirit, whom He poured out upon us richly through Jesus Christ our Savior.

And in 2 Corinthians 5:17 Paul says:

Therefore, if anyone is in Christ, he is a new creation; the old has gone, the new has come! (NIV)

If we are in Christ, we are not part old and part new. If that is who we are Paul would have said it. *We are new.*

A new creation is something new that has been brought into existence. God doesn't renovate, He innovates. We have not been "rehabilitated."

We have been re-created. This is our new state and identity in Christ. It is this mindset that we must adopt daily to keep from falling into old, entrapping behaviors, or coming under the dictates of spiritual leaders who do not know how to lead us to real life and freedom.

Conclusion

Knowing that God must intervene because we need to be made new, and asking Him to intervene is one thing. It is another thing to believe He has done it and to understand what that means in practice. Most of us have a hard time allowing these truths to refeed and permeate and transform us from within, because we simply have too much flesh-and-blood evidence to the contrary. Keeping our eyes on the evidence of "things above" seems to be the biggest struggle—and not only for people who have been spiritually abused, but for every Christian.

We will look more at the real fight of faith in the next chapter.

Spiritual abuse has the effect of making people extremely self-focused, preoccupied with doing things right and keeping happy those who are in places of authority. Recovery begins and continues with keeping our focus on God, what He has done, and who we are because of that. And in the context of open, grace-full relationships, this focus can be maintained.

19

Recovering Right Focus

A number of years ago, my wife awakened one night at 2:00 A.M. to the smell of smoke (Jeff speaking). A thick cloud hung halfway from the ceiling to the floor. She shook me awake, then made a beeline for the kids' rooms to get them up. We grabbed a few sleeping bags, called the fire department, and headed for our car, which was parked out in the February air.

In a short time, a siren broke the black, predawn silence and a fire truck screeched to a halt in front of our house. A half-dozen men, looking like huge yellow astronauts, rushed into the house. Dressed in their vast array of bulky equipment, they looked twice their normal size.

We expected the house to burst into flames any minute as we waited in the cold car for the firefighters to do their jobs. No fire. Not even any smoke. Just cold. Still we waited.

"I think I'll go in and check out what's happening," I volunteered, after a long time. "Save the baby pictures," I heard Holly say as I made my way through the cold.

Inside, it was silent as a ghost town. There were no firefighters to be seen. Eventually, I found them in the basement. What I saw gave me great relief—and nearly made me laugh.

Six very uncomfortable firefighters were crouched in our basement: The ceiling was only five-and-a-half feet high. One of them said, "We found the culprit." The smoke that had chased us into the cold night was caused by the furnace's cold air intake motor, which had burned out. Electrical fumes and smoke had poured into the ductwork and made their way into every room of the house. As they told me this I noticed that beside the furnace, "fighting" the fire, was one gargantuan firefighter, wearing helmet, slicker, oxygen tank, boots, ax and wielding . . . an ice cream bucket. Yes, he had filled an old ice cream bucket with water from the laundry sink, and was crouched over, flicking handfuls of water onto the red-hot intake motor, the water hissing as it turned into steam.

He's a little overdressed for this job, I thought, smiling to myself in relief.

Much later I thought about this incident, and somehow it reminded me, oddly, of the church. Here we are with all of our equipment: The God of the Universe is our Father, and He is on our side; Jesus Christ is our Lord, Friend, Brother, Shepherd and Physician, and His cross defeated the enemy for all time; the Holy Spirit lives in us and equips us with supplies from our Father to live and fight the Christian life; our value and acceptance is a settled issue; we are offered a supernatural quality of life here and now—and a life that lasts forever.

And yet, of course, there is another side.

Satan has erected fortresses in people's lives through incest, child abuse, domestic violence, alcoholism and countless other addictions, spiritual abuse—*any* way he can deceive, rob and enslave. But instead of tearing down these fortresses with truth and grace, the church has fought about the color of the hymnals. We have taught classes, built buildings, served on committees, and gone to seminars so that our leaders can feel spiritually gratified. We have spent our spiritual energy bribing our children to go to church and memorize Bible verses by promising them perfect attendance pins and trophies. We have taken each others' spiritual inventories to make sure people aren't going to movies, wearing makeup, or chewing gum in church. We have taught people prayer recipes and formulas. If this is really our job, we are truly spiritually overdressed.

Have we lost our focus? Have we left behind our true job of leading people into the grace and real empowerment that comes from dwelling simply, honestly, closely with God? Do we keep adding to the "good news" until it's not good anymore?

We believe this is so.

Some Possible Explanations

Many things might explain the loss of simple focus prevalent in so many churches. One explanation is that not everyone who goes to church is a Christian. A Christian is someone whose life is from God because of Christ. Adhering to a set of doctrines, or excluding those who don't, does not make anyone a Christian. Hence, one of the reasons churches or people who are in them look so dead, perhaps, is that they have so little of the real life of God flowing through them. Consequently, a church or person may neglect the real needs of people and focus on performance, doctrines, how things look, buildings, parking lots, and increased attendance figures, all because the natural and temporal is all they have.

Another reason may be that the church has become ill, a storehouse for the unresolved issues of those who attend, an image-bearer of the members' dysfunctional families of origin. This is what happens when the "can't-talk" rule from a family system reproduces itself in a spiritual system. You can't get well from problems you can't admit you have. Therefore, you keep the same problems and bring them into your next relationship system. And when leaders sweep away their own or others' problems, attitudes and questions under the facade of a "be happy" spirituality, or when they try to drive out problems with rules and formulas, the result is that whole churches get sick.

When the Church Acts as the Body

The New Testament uses the Greek word for "one another" over fifty times to describe the relationship dynamic between Christians in the body of Christ. It is what is called a "reciprocal" pronoun, which means that both parties involved will benefit from a particular action because both are doing it. "Comfort one another" means that both parties will be comforted because both are comforting. "Love one another" means that both will experience love because both are loving. "Encourage one another" means that both will be encouraged because both are encouraging.

The "one anothers" in the New Testament communicate God's intention for us to be involved in each other's lives. Every "one another" is there for the purpose of helping us grow stronger spiritually as a result of functioning in relationship with other members of the body of Christ. The foundation of spiritual maturity is dependence upon God alone as the Source of all life. The foundation is strengthened by deep relationships growing out of involvement with others, openness toward them, and interdependency upon these fellow members of Christ's body. Conversely, shutting down discussion, not allowing questions, and force-feeding doctrines brings about a closed, isolated and spiritually sick environment.

That is to say, when the church acts as the body of Christ, it becomes a "safe place" in the midst of a hostile world. When it becomes a spiritual trap, it is something else—for some, it can feel like hell on earth.

In 2 Corinthians 5:20 Paul calls us "ambassadors for Christ." An ambassador is the highest ranking representative of one country to another. In times of hostility between the two countries, the ambassador is a representative of the "safe place" in the middle of an unsafe place. The embassy and the land it is on is the sovereign territory of the ambassador's home government. If you are trapped in unfriendly territory and can make it to the embassy, it's like being in a piece of your home country.

This world is not our home. In Ephesians 2:19, Paul says we are "fellow citizens with the saints, and are of God's household." Paul also says in Philippians 3:20, "Our citizenship is in heaven." We live in hostile territory. In 1 Peter 2:11 it says, "Beloved, I urge you as aliens and strangers. . . ." We are God's ambassadors, representatives of the safe place in the middle of the unsafe place.

Hebrews 4:15–16 says:

> For we do not have a high priest who cannot sympathize with our weaknesses, but one who has been tempted in all things as we are, yet without sin. Let us therefore draw near with confidence to the throne of grace, that we may receive mercy and may find grace to help in time of need.

Our Father is the sympathetic King who has sent us abroad. The Throne of Grace is the safe place we represent. The church needs to be a safe place for people who need to find grace to help in time of need. "Let no unwholesome [literally, "rotten"] word proceed from your mouth, but only such a word as is good for edification according to the need of the moment, *that it may give grace to those who hear*" (Ephesians 4:29).

Churches where tired, wounded people are given formulas and advice to help in time of need, or are shamed for having a need, do not represent the true King.

Our Job

We have made a great deal of effort to expose performance-oriented Christianity as one significant root of the problem of spiritual abuse. As we have made plain, we see this as nothing short of a complete lack of understanding about the true life in Christ that comes by grace.

Let's consider that life of grace now.

John 11 contains the marvelously moving account of Jesus raising His friend Lazarus from the dead. News had come from Bethany that Lazarus was sick. Instead of rushing to his friend's side, Jesus waited an extra two days before leaving for Bethany. When He arrived, Lazarus had already been dead and in the tomb four days. Four days is significant because of a Jewish belief that the spirit of the dead person hovered around the body for three days and then left. Lazarus was officially dead.

After hearing what happened from Lazarus' sisters, Mary and Martha, Jesus reassured them and asked some bystanders to take the stone away from in front of the cave that served as his tomb. After they removed it Jesus said a prayer. We will pick up the story at John 11:43.

> And when He had said these things, He cried out with a loud voice, "Lazarus, come forth." He who had died came forth, bound hand and foot with wrappings; and his face was wrapped around with a cloth. Jesus said to them, "Unbind him, and let him go."

Picture the spectators as they struggled to move the stone from the front of the tomb. Couldn't Jesus—with power from heaven to raise people from the dead—have used that same power to roll the stone away himself? Undoubtedly. Could Jesus have transported Lazarus out of the cave? Of course. Now picture the mummified Lazarus, struggling out of the tomb into the bright sunlight. Couldn't Jesus have caused the grave clothes to drop off? Why didn't He?

We believe He had a purpose in His actions—and in what He left for His followers to do. Only Jesus can bring *life* to dead churches, families, marriages, or people. That is His job. Once there is life, however, there are still the grave clothes of shame and self-righteousness, old views of ourselves and God, and the unhealthy ways of having relationships to be changed. And then there is that nasty tendency to keep trying to get the life we already have from things that cannot give life—which is the process that leads back to shame or self-righteousness. The church needs to be a safe place in which we begin to peel away the grave clothes that keep reborn people from being able to act alive. That is our job. Jesus has left that up to us.

There is another interesting aspect to this story. If Lazarus had emerged from the tomb without the grave clothes he would have been naked, also true if Jesus had caused the grave clothes to drop off.

This would have caused him a great deal of humiliation and shame from being exposed. By having those around unwrap Lazarus, Jesus was providing an opportunity for people close to him to help him lose the grave clothes but not lose his dignity. Likewise, we in the body of Christ need to help one another get free from our spiritual, psychological and emotional grave clothes. But we need to do it in a way that respects the process and protects the dignity of people.

The Word of God cries out to us that mercy and grace from God are the only true source of life, value and acceptance. Faith is the only way to receive it. It is only available as a gift based on Christ's performance. Every other message calls us to pursue life and meaning as if it comes from what we have, or what we do or don't do. It is a serious matter to be lured into attempting to find life from negative, empty behaviors. It is more serious, however, to be decoyed into positive, spiritual-looking endeavors. This can be very difficult to spot, and even more difficult to confront. And what a calamity when these wrong-focused messages come from Christian families or churches.

Therefore, we believe it is imperative to refocus victims of spiritual abuse on the truth about God and His "good news." For this reason, we offer a list of "reminders," from the heart of God as follows:

God loves us a great deal: "See how great a love the Father has bestowed upon us, that we should be called children of God; and such we are" (1 John 3:1).

He is extravagant with His grace: "To the praise of the glory of His grace, which He freely bestowed on us in the Beloved . . . according to the riches of His grace, which He lavished upon us" (Ephesians 1:6–8).

He makes us stand: "Now He who establishes us with you in Christ and anointed us is God, who also sealed us and gave us the Spirit in our hearts as a pledge" (2 Corinthians 1:21–22).

He can be trusted: "Let us hold fast the confession of our hope without wavering, for He who promised is faithful" (Hebrews 10:23).

We have been made entirely new: "Knowing this, that our old self was crucified with Him . . ." (Romans 6:6). "Therefore if anyone is in Christ, he is a new creation" (2 Corinthians 5:17, NIV).

We have been handpicked: "Just as He chose us in Him before the foundation of the world . . ." (Ephesians 1:4).

We are blameless in his sight: ". . . that we should be holy and blameless before Him" (Ephesians 1:4).

What is His is already ours: "We have obtained an inheritance" (Ephesians 1:11), because "The Spirit Himself bears witness with our spirit that we are children of God, and if children, heirs also, heirs of God and fellow heirs with Christ" (Romans 8:16–17).

God is not keeping track: "And their sins and their lawless deeds I will remember no more" (Hebrews 10:17).

He doesn't have a problem with our struggles and pain: "Blessed be the God and Father of our Lord Jesus Christ, the Father of mercies and God of all comfort; who comforts us in all our affliction . . ." (2 Corinthians 1:3–4).

We don't need to improve on what He's done: "In Him you have been made complete" (Colossians 2:10), and "Hence, also, He is able to save completely those who draw near to God through Him" (Hebrews 7:25).

When we fail, Jesus defends us: "Since He always lives to make intercession for them" (Hebrews 7:25), and "If anyone sins, we have an Advocate with the Father, Jesus Christ the righteous" (1 John 2:1).

Learning to Live All Over Again

In Philippians 3, Paul says, ". . . let us keep living by that same standard to which we have attained" (v. 16). He does not say, "Live to attain the standard." He says, "We have attained it." As we have seen already in our study of the Law, there is no way we can attain the standard by trying to be good standard-attainers. We meet the standard because we are in Christ.

In Galatians 6, Paul says, "For neither is circumcision anything, nor uncircumcision, but a new creation. And those who will walk by this rule, peace and mercy be upon them" (vv. 15–16). The word "rule" in Greek does not mean law or precept. It means "ruler" or "measuring stick." Paul is telling us new creations to live like new creations. He is saying that peace and mercy go to those who measure up to the new creation yardstick. This is accomplished by being in Christ, not by trying hard to measure up.

Living Consistently

Earlier we talked about the person who attempts to erase shame, to earn acceptance, and to establish a positive self-concept based on his or her own behaviors. This is the person's motive for acting or not acting certain ways. It is a different story for those who are in Christ.

Since there is "now no condemnation for those who are in Christ Jesus," and since we are already new, accepted, and complete in Him, we are free to live for a different motive. As Paul says in 2 Corinthians 5, "For the love of Christ controls us" (v. 14). Instead of earning, proving, or pleasing, we can do what we do *just because Jesus loves us and we love Him.*

We used to believe that the successful Christian life was about *doing* good, and not doing sins. But sin is more than a behavior issue; sin results when we forget to trust in the real God for our identity and spiritual strength, or when we place our trust in something other than our Source.

If I use drugs, steal, or commit adultery in an attempt to meet my needs it is sin. What makes it sin is *not* that I performed a behavior on the "bad list"—although I did do that. The sin is that I tried to draw life or significance from something that could not give it. Instead of trusting God I trusted a false god. That is missing the mark.

If, on the other hand, I teach a Sunday school class, serve on a committee or put money in the offering in order to validate myself or earn approval from God or someone else, it's also a sin. What is a sin about it, however, is not that I didn't do behaviors on the "good list" (because I did do them). It's that I tried to draw life and significance from something that could not give it. Instead of trusting God I turned to a false god—*positive-looking*, but false just the same. That also is missing the mark.

Whenever I become aware of a sin—a behavior resulting from looking to my own performance instead of to what Jesus did on the Cross—there is no shame. It is no final "proof" that I am unworthy of God's grace and empowerment because I have temptation or I have sinned. It simply means that for a time, I again attempted to draw "life" out of wrong sources and actions. It is the process of the Christian life to reteach my mind and soul how to rest in the promise of Life itself.

I do this, first of all, by responding to guilt as a "spiritual nerve-ending." Guilt tells me I am headed toward death, not toward God and life. I then go to God and say I'm sorry. He forgives me. It is over. I may still have to live with some consequences of my behaviors. But I do not have to hide from God. And I do not have to scramble around, trying to fix my life in order to earn back spiritual points that I lost: There were no points. My struggle is still the same: to hang on to Jesus, and to live consistent with who I am and what I have in Him. If I remember who I am and what I have and my behavior hits the mark, there is no self-righteousness. I feel grateful. I go to God and say, "Thank you."

The Way We First Got Life

In Colossians 2, Paul says, "As you therefore have received Christ Jesus the Lord, so walk in Him" (v. 6).

Walk the same way you came in! We did not come into our relationship with Jesus on the basis of good behaviors. We did not earn God's approval by trying hard. We trusted in Jesus and received a gift. Continue looking to Jesus as the basis of your vindication and validation. The Christian life really is, first and foremost, a struggle to simply, purely, "trust in God."

Continue to rest, we say, as you did in the beginning of your Christian walk, in what God has done and promises to do.

This is the focus of our true "spiritual battle." How many of us—after years of trying and failing—need to come to simply rest in Him?

His invitation is still, *"Come to Me...."*

For many people trying to decide whether to leave or stay in an abusive religious system, the question is just too close to home. Many factors cloud the issue. Consider the following perspectives in order to gain a clearer view of the issues. With a more objective picture you will be able to make the decision that is best for the system, your family and yourself.

20

One Response: Flight

Don sank low in his chair as he poured out a painful story. He had been the pastor of a growing suburban church for six years. Things went along smoothly until one day, about four years into his ministry there, when he began to learn some things about himself.

Foremost, he realized that much of what he was doing was motivated by a need for people's approval. This also found its way into his relationship with his wife and kids. He noticed that even though most people in the church were pleased with how things were going, a certain group was not happy no matter what happened. Despite the fact that the church's progress was ahead of his own five-year plan, he noticed less and less joy in doing the very thing to which he had dedicated his life. And he was getting tired.

He decided to get help working through some of these issues. During his course of counseling he saw that most of his ministry and family issues were simply a result of living out the effects of having grown up in a performance-based Christian family. He also recognized that, for a person who had been around the church his whole life and whose job it was to communicate God's grace, he had never really experienced it himself.

As time passed, grace "sank in," and became more precious and liberating with each counseling session. One day, he realized that it was this deeper understanding of God's grace that had set him free to do the painful work of looking inside. His attitudes about life and ministry were being transformed, almost automatically. And his preaching changed, too.

The response to his new sermons, however, was becoming a problem. To one group of people—the wounded and tired majority—the messages about God's unconditional love, the true identity of the believer, and the ability to be honest about pain and struggles came like a cool drink in the desert. These folks loved grace, and they responded with a level of openness and honesty never seen before in this church. Wounds began to heal. Families began to mend. To the other group—the powerful minority—it sounded like permission to be lazy or to act irresponsible.

Don began to feel resistance; not directly at first, but in the form of "constructive criticism." People began to tell him that they liked him better before. "Could you just go back to the way you were?" It intensified into nit-picking the words he used in the sermons. A campaign was organized to call for a vote of confidence (one of several that eventually occurred) that came out easily in his favor. Some of those most adversarial even left the church—although they continued to send messages of disagreement through those who stayed. Finally, Don got a letter from the former board chairman asking for his resignation.

"Do you think I should just leave?" he asked.

How Do You Decide?

How do you decide whether to leave or stay in a spiritually abusive system? How can you tell if it is more helpful to stay, or more helpful to the situation for you to leave? Should our response be to *fight*? Or should it be *flight*?

In the interest of helping you decide, please take some time to honestly answer the following questions about your present situation.

We will tell you before you start that, in our opinion, there is no neat checklist you can use to help you decide. In the end you have to pay attention to what is going on in and around you, and listen especially to what God tells you to do. Listening to God is up to you. The questions that follow are our attempt to help you better pay attention to what is going on. They are based on some of the lessons God taught us as we were faced with this very same question early in our ministry together.

Please consider the following ideas concerning the question of whether to stay or leave your spiritually abusive system. You may find that they free you to leave the abusive system, if that's what you decide you need to do.

Does grace really have a chance?

God can intervene in an abusive system anytime He wants. And sometimes He does. Recently some friends of ours moved to a small town quite a distance away. Not long after, they became involved with a legalistic church where leaders dominated most aspects of everyday life. When our friends confronted the situation, no one seemed to be listening. They called to say they left that church and after a little searching had found one that was more grace-full. What is interesting is that just recently we received a call from the pastor of the church they left. He wanted us to send every tape, book, or article we could on the topic of "grace."

Because God is in charge, grace always has a chance. But . . .

Situations do not always turn around. In light of that, here is a rule of thumb to help you decide if it is wise to stay: If the leadership is grace-full—even with a group of very legalistic sheep—grace has a chance. Sheep tend to follow shepherds.

If, however, there is a bottleneck of power-posturing leaders at the top, who are performance-oriented, the chances of things changing are very slim. Once again, sheep follow shepherds. And those who do not leave will tend to become entrenched in domination and legalism, whatever form those take. If this is the case, you should probably leave.

Are you supporting what you hate?

By staying and contributing your time, money and energy, are you helping something continue when, honestly in your heart, you disagree with it? We believe that if everyone who was doing this would stop, many very unhealthy and abusive organizations would be unable to continue functioning. We also believe that if there was no such person as God, many religious places would not miss a beat.

As I said before, when I first got out of seminary (Jeff speaking), I worked in an inpatient treatment center. When I started working there it was a healthy place for employees and an amazing healing environment for patients. After a while, however, the focus changed from leading people to emotional honesty and health, and it became more important to keep our patient census up. The center began letting in and keeping people who needed to be somewhere else. In addition, unethical care was given. Teenage female clients were being given breast examinations by the doctor, who was not there to give physicals of any kind. He also prescribed mood-altering substances for colds. And we were a chemical dependency treatment center!

A number of the counselors went to the director of the treatment center and told him what was going on. We voiced our concern that the doctor was unethical and incompetent. The director replied, "We don't want a competent doctor. We just want a doctor that signs everything we put in front of him."

Where do you go from there?

Things got worse each day. Being with fifteen clients who didn't want to be there was easier than being around most of the staff. The other staff members and I spent more time behind closed doors solving agency issues than we did working with the clients. I kept confronting the system. And every time I confronted something, I was told that the problem was me.

Every day before I went in to work, I would actually cry and complain. I hated it. But every day I went there anyway: I gave my energy and most of my waking hours to something with which I didn't agree. My wife would try to put me back together again, and remind me of what I was there for. But I couldn't think about that. I just wanted the system to change, because if it changed I'd be a happy person once again.

It occurred to me during this time that, really, I was a slave. I had an adequate salary, a pension and my health insurance. But instead of these things serving me, *I was serving them*. And I did this at the expense of my integrity, not to mention my emotional health.

For the system there was no problem. I was the problem because I broke the "can't-talk" rule. But you see, in a sense the director was right. I *was* the problem. I could do absolutely nothing about the problems with the system. But there was one thing I could do something about: Me—I could stop supporting something I hated and thought was wrong, though it would cost me a lot.

I resigned.

If you find that you have been supporting something with your life that you hate with your heart—there is something you can change. You can change you.

Do you need to be right?

Then there is the issue of being right. There were a total of nine people who left the treatment center about the same time I did. For a long time before we left, every one of us struggled with this question: "If we are right, why do *we* have to leave?" All this question did, however, was to keep nine "right" people supporting a system that we detested.

Can you stay, and stay healthy, both at the same time?

This is probably one of the most important questions you can ask. Losing your spiritual, not to mention physical, emotional and psychological health is not worth the cost. Neither is stressing-out your family, or neglecting them to take on a dysfunctional system. Many children of spiritual-abuse victims suffer neglect because their parents are so preoccupied with trying to carry along a collapsing church.

One person described what happened to him this way. "It felt like I was hanging on to the ship of our church with one hand and the pier of spiritual health and reality with the other. I hung on tighter and tighter as the ship began to pull away from the dock. In the end I had to let go of the ship and climb back onto the pier. But in the meantime, my spiritual arms felt like they had been pulled from their sockets."

Look at the following diagram to see how you could lose your integrity and become an emotional and spiritual mess. *A* in the inside circle represents your views and feelings on the inside. The *B*s represent those of the people in the system with which you disagree. The jagged lines are the tension between the two views.

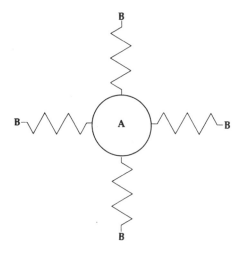

You may decide to put on external *B*s in order to alleviate the tension and maintain "peace and unity" among the brethren. That would look like the following diagram.

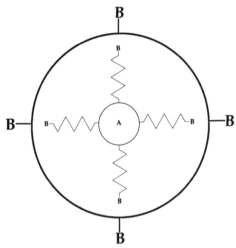

Notice from the straight lines that the tension, at least on the surface, has been resolved. Notice, too, that there are now jagged lines between you and you—that is, between your heart on the inside, and your actions on the outside.

Here is the point. If you have an *A* on the inside, you *should* be at odds with the *B*s on the outside. This is called integrity. In order to stay in an environment like this and stay well, you will need a lot of support. Being in this kind of stress won't make you sick if you are well supported by healthy people. But incongruity with who you really are will eventually make you sick at heart and in spirit.

Avoid looking at others to see what to do. Don't take a poll. If you take a poll, it might come out different than what your heart is telling you. Then you would have to pretend your heart is telling you something different in order to erase the tension with the results of the poll.

If you find that staying in the system is costing you your own spiritual and emotional health, or the health of those you love, you should leave.

Can you decide your own limits—and stick with them?

Set limits as to how much of yourself you are willing to invest without seeing healthy changes. This will help prevent you from being sucked into an equity-rescuing scenario. *Then stick to your limit.* That's another reason you need to stay in close touch with people who can help hold you accountable. This is not the same as taking a poll. It is simply getting encouragement in order to be able to do what you already decided to do.

While they are reminding you that you are not insane, and that you are not the problem, they can remind you about how you felt and what you said when you first set your limits. In an unhealthy system, it is easy to forget.

If you need to, refer to the equity diagram we pictured earlier. From now on, measure how much you have invested from point *0* on the line, not from the last place of investment. Start counting the costs from honesty and health, not from the last compromise you made. Leave when you have come to your set limit.

Do you believe God cares more about the church than you do?

If you have come from a shame-based family system, you probably struggle with feeling a responsibility to be involved in fixing every problem. This will make it hard to leave any place where the problems still are not solved. Just remember that however much you care about the church, God cares about His church even more. And He can fix it even without you. Do you believe that?

Then there is the issue of how much God needs us. Many people have been given this line of reasoning in order to get them involved in any number of religious endeavors: "If I don't do it who will?" "God needs you." Jesus said, "I will build my church." He can and will do it, with or without us.

And what about the "truth" and "justice" issues? "If you leave, who will see that justice is served? Who will make sure that those who remain hear the truth?" Psalm 89:14 says, "Righteousness and justice are the foundation of Thy throne. Lovingkindness and truth go before Thee." You see, God cares about these issues, too, and He will resolve injustices and expose lies.

Is it possible the system might need to die?

In Revelation 3, John writes to the church at Sardis, "I know your deeds, that you have a name that you are alive, but you are dead" (v. 1). Sometimes staying in a spiritually abusive system, instead of being helpful, simply props up its facade as a healthy, non-abusive system. Others may be thinking, "It can't be that bad. If it *was* that bad, people would leave—right?" This type of reasoning insulates false leadership from accountability. Leaving does not kill a dead system, it just makes it look as dead as it is.

There are times God writes *Ichabod*, "the glory of the Lord has departed," on the door and leaves. There are times when it is the best thing for you to leave, as well. After all, do you want to be in a church that God has left?

Are you trying to help the system, even though you are exhausted?

If so, you are no longer resting in God. Find a place where it is absolutely fine for you to simply rest and receive for a while. In a spiritually abusive system, permission to rest will never be granted. Your cries for help will be labeled unspiritual. It is ludicrous to think you can help someone else to find rest when you yourself have been spiritually annihilated.

Are you able to listen to the voice of sanity?

You can probably find that voice by reconnecting with the people who already left the system, because they saw what you now see. Perhaps there are a whole group of former friends you used to trust before they left. But when they began confronting things and warning you, you thought they were the problem. And the system told you to stay away from them, so you did. Look them up. Find the people who were caring and gracious to you before they left—the ones who respected your decision to stay. Chances are they will be kind and gracious again.

Do you really know where to sow?

In Mark 4, Jesus taught His disciples how to be good sowers. The lesson concerns various kinds of soil. There are four kinds: the soil next to the road; the thorny soil; the rocky soil; and the good soil. Seeds that land on the shoulder of the road don't amount to anything. Neither do the ones that land in the thorns or on the rocky place. The seeds that yield a harvest are the ones that land on the good soil.

Now, if you were a sower who caught Jesus' meaning, where would you try to sow your seeds? On the good soil, of course. And where would you try to avoid sowing seeds altogether? It's obvious. On the other soils. In the parable, the seeds that landed on these other soils did so by accident. No one would sow good seeds in bad soils on purpose.

As you try to confront your spiritually abusive system with truth, do you find that truth won't be received? This is *not* because you didn't speak the truth long enough, or well enough. It might be because you are sowing your truth on rocks. When you realize that rocks cannot grow, it is best to find soil that will. "And whoever does not receive you, nor heed your words, as you go out of that house or that city, shake off the dust of your feet" (Matthew 10:14).

If you came today for the first time, knowing what you now know about the system, would you stay?

If the answer is no, then why are you continuing to return?

Song for the Spiritually Abused

Before we look at the other option—to fight—we would like to offer this song for those who have been abused in the church. It is, among other things, a cry and a prayer.

"Stretch Out Your Hand"
by Dan Adler

1. Lord, you are God, Maker of the universe.
   Lord, by your hand you formed the land and sea.
   Now you have called us to bring your truth to all the earth,
   So with one voice we humbly call on Thee.

Chorus:
Stretch out your hand to heal
With signs and wonders reveal
Your mighty power and your glory in this land
Be mindful of our pain
Give boldness to proclaim
The glorious gospel of grace! Stretch out your hand.

2. Lord, when you walked among the people of the earth,
   You touched the lame and caused the blind to see.
   Now you have made us your body here upon the earth,
   So now we pray, "Come touch the world through me."

Bridge:
As the nations rage around us,
Lord, we come to seek your face.
Come and fill us with your Spirit
By your power shake this place.[1]

---

[1]Copyright © 1991, Dan Adler. Used by permission.

Having learned everything you have, you may believe that you should stay and help the system. If you do, don't be naive. Telling the truth will mean a fight. Be sure that it is God who is telling you to stay, and that you are not staying for the wrong reasons.

21

A Second Response: Fight

After considering the questions in the last chapter, you may still sense that God is leading you to stay in the abusive system. If that is true, here are some reminders to help you fight the fight you are going to face.

Decide whom you serve.

The issue is not *whether* we will serve someone, it is *who*.

Not long ago my wife Holly and I (Jeff speaking) met a senior high girl who was suffering from anorexia. Among the factors contributing to her illness was the fact that her father was forcing her to commit incest with him. We asked if she had ever received any help, but she had not. We asked if we could approach her pastor on her behalf. She gave us her permission.

We sought out the pastor, told him our concerns, and asked him if he could get involved with her and her family. This was his answer: "I've been at this church for about five years now. It's been rough for most of that time. Resistant people, no money, lack of involvement on the part of the congregation. Last year things seemed to turn around. Giving went up. Attendance went up. This man has been very active in the church, long before I ever got there. If I confront this problem, I'll lose my ministry."

Too late! He had already lost his ministry. This pastor *served* an incestuous father, money, attendance figures, and the ministry.

"Let a man regard us in this manner," says Paul in 1 Corinthians 4:1, "*as servants of Christ.*" You cannot serve people and Jesus both at the same time. If your perspective is that you are here to serve people, you may *please* people, but you might not *serve* them. If your perspective is that you are here to serve Christ, you will *serve* people, but you might not *please* them. Each of us must decide which we will do. This pastor served "in the name of Jesus," but he didn't serve Jesus.

Be Wise About the Battle

If you decide to stay, don't be naive. There is going to be tension. And there will be a fight, too—first, on the inside of you, and possibly on the outside, as well. Here are some things you should know about that fight.

Be ready for resistance.

In Acts 4, we see the account of Peter and John healing a man who was lame for forty years. Their authority was baffling to the religious leaders because Peter and John were "uneducated and untrained men" (v. 13). Here was the dilemma: The disciples had not done or said something with which the leaders took issue, but God's power exhibited through John and Peter made the trained and educated leaders, who had the power position, look powerless. They *postured* authority; Peter and John *had* authority.

Then came the resistance. They were arrested, and a "can't-talk" rule was imposed: " 'But in order that it may not spread any further among the people, let us warn them to speak no more to any man in this name.' And when they had summoned them, they commanded them not to speak or teach at all in the name of Jesus" (vv. 17–18). When they kept talking, the threats grew worse. This brings us to the next point.

Keep telling the truth.

In Acts 4:19, Peter and John respond: "Whether it is right in the sight of God to give heed to you rather than God, you be the judge; for we cannot stop speaking what we have seen and heard." Look also at Acts 5:27–29:

> And when they had brought them, they stood them before the Council. And the high priest questioned them, saying, "We gave you strict orders not to continue teaching in this name, and behold, you have filled Jerusalem with your teaching." . . . But Peter and the apostles answered and said, "We must obey God rather than men."

As we have noted, in abusive systems there is double-talk, and things are said "in code." In order to stay out of trouble, you have to become good at encoding and decoding. Therefore, another reason you will get in trouble for telling the truth is that *truth actually breaks the codes*. Saying things straight makes the crooked things look crooked. Let me illustrate.

When I first came to Church of the Open Door (Jeff speaking), I attended a business meeting. I was not even an official member, but I wanted to see what went on. The topic being discussed was whether the church should spend money on a certain item. A woman stood up to take the floor. I found out much later that she exerted a great deal of crooked control in the church through her three family members who were on the board. Here is what happened:

"There are a lot of people in the church who don't think we should be spending money that way," she said. I looked around the room, which had become deathly silent. With that one sentence she had shut down the discussion. Now I had just come from working in a treatment center where we spent almost all of our time helping people learn how to be honest and straight. The message to the addicted was "Get honest or die!" This didn't look honest to me.

"Who?" I asked. (Was it possible? The room grew more deathly still.) I had dared to question. Almost everyone turned around to look at me. Then they turned back to see the woman's response.

"A *lot* of people," she said, her voice betraying a tone of indignation.

"Where are they?" I asked.

"They're not here. They didn't come," she said. She was turning red with anger.

"Well, do you have that opinion? Do you personally think the church should not spend money that way?" I asked.

She answered with no hesitation. "No, of course not."

"Then perhaps the reason these other people didn't come," I said, "is that they have you to run messages for them—messages that you don't even agree with."

This woman was speaking out-of-line, presenting a coded, crooked message. She had used the missing "them" to run the church for years. After the meeting another person came up to me, and with a shaming tone of voice tried to impose the "can't-talk" rule. "The reason people don't come to meetings is because of people like *you!*"

Where does the strength come from to be able to take this kind of stand? The Word of God gives us several answers.

First, there is strength in the truth. "We cannot stop speaking what we have seen and heard." We have heard people in recovery say this same kind of thing. Here is the way they tend to say it: "Since I have been in counseling I have learned so much about how dysfunctional I was and how abusive my family/church was. I've seen and heard too much, and the truth of this has set me free to look at my issues and move on in my life. I can't go back."

Second, there is strength in having decided whom you serve and to whom you are accountable. In Acts 4:29, the disciples refer to themselves as *bond-servants*. Bond-servants were not people who were brought into captivity and forced to serve. They were people who *sold themselves* into the service of a master. They had decided whom they served.

This still begs the question: *Where does the strength to stand come from?* Paul says in 1 Corinthians 4:3–4:

> But to me it is a very small thing that I should be examined by you, or by any human court; in fact, I do not even examine myself. I am conscious of nothing against myself, yet I am not by this acquitted; but the one who examines me is the Lord.

Paul is not saying, "I don't have to listen to anyone." He is simply saying that when all is said and done, we have to receive our final approval from God, something, by the way, that we already have!

Never run messages for other people. Carrying on the confrontation on behalf of others conveys to those in charge that things are not as bad as they are. It also allows for a lesser degree of accountability on their part. Instead of having to deal with the confrontations of many people, they only have to deal with yours. Second, you will be allowing people to vent their tension on you, thus enabling them to avoid facing the right person. Third, you will be helping others to remain stuck in the dysfunctional communication skills they learned in past relationships: People need to learn to act as if their opinion matters. Finally, *you will get very tired*.

Know who your enemy is.

Ephesians 6:12 says:

> For our struggle is not against flesh and blood, but against the rulers, against the powers, against the world forces of this darkness, against the spiritual forces of wickedness in the heavenly places.

And 2 Corinthians 10:3 says, "For though we walk in the flesh, we do not war according to the flesh." People are not our enemy; Satan is the enemy.

It is true, however, that Satan uses people sometimes. Galatians 2:4 tells us that the false brethren "had been sneaked in." In Matthew 13, Jesus tells a parable of a landowner who sowed good seed in his field. But during the night "his enemy came and sowed tares also among the wheat" (v. 25). Satan oversows what God has sown. While people are sometimes used as pawns, they are not the enemy.

This means that we do not have to overrate the power that people have. Remember that the man behind the curtain is just a man. In addition, we don't have to *underrate* the power that is ours. Acts 1:8 says, "But you shall receive power when the Holy Spirit has come upon you." As a Christian you have that Spirit, as is clear from Romans 8:9: "If anyone does not have the Spirit of Christ, he does not belong to Him." And look again at 2 Corinthians 10:4, where Paul says, "For the weapons of our warfare are not of the flesh, but divinely powerful for the destruction of fortresses."

Hang On to the Shepherd.

In Matthew 10, Jesus sent the disciples to the lost sheep in the house of Israel. He said, "Behold, I send you out as sheep in the midst of wolves" (v. 16).

We are sent *to* sheep, *as* sheep, *among* wolves. How does a sheep among the wolves minister, or even survive for that matter? The answer is a strong shepherd to depend upon.

Rising up in anger is *not* necessary or helpful. In fact, the opposite is true. In 2 Corinthians 12:9–10 Paul says:

And He has said to me, "My grace is sufficient for you, for power is perfected in weakness." Most gladly, therefore, I will rather boast about my weaknesses, that the power of Christ may dwell in me . . . for when I am weak, then I am strong.

Isaiah 40:29–31 says:

He gives strength to the weary, and to him who lacks might He increases power. Though youths grow weary and tired, and vigorous young men stumble badly, yet those who wait for the Lord will gain new strength; they will mount up with wings like eagles, they will run and not get tired, they will walk and not become weary.

Fighting the fight of faith does not mean getting aggressive. It does not take money, status, an education, or the ability to speak. It takes dependence upon God. Just hang on to God, and tell the truth. This is God's fight.

Messes Are Not Bad

Churches are messy simply because of the fact that they are relationship systems made up of many different kinds of people. If you start to say things out loud in a system where the "can't-talk" rule has reigned, more of the mess will be evident. And you will get the blame. But the truth never causes the mess, it just exposes it. In fact, messes aren't "bad." They serve a very important purpose.

In 1 Corinthians 11:18–19, Paul says to a very contentious Corinthian church:

> For, in the first place, when you come together as a church, I hear that divisions exist among you; and in part, I believe it. For there must also be factions among you.

There *must* be factions and divisions? What about peace at all costs? What good thing could ever come from divisions in the church? Paul answers: "In order that those who are approved may have become evident among you" (v. 19). Only in the midst of division will you be able to tell who genuinely cares about God and His ways from the heart. Don't leave just because there is a mess. Messes can be good.

Confront the leaven.

Churches and families are relationship systems made up of interrelated, interdependent parts. Because of this, what is going on with one part affects the others. "A little leaven leavens the whole lump," is the way Paul said it. The leaven to which he was referring in Galatians 5:9 was legalism.

If you are going to be part of a healthy church, you will need to confront the leaven, even if there is just a little. Remember, "a *little* leaven leavens the whole lump." How much more is it necessary to confront the leaven if you decide to stay in a spiritually abusive church, where there is a lot of leaven?

Know how a healthy spiritual system functions.

An unhealthy system is one in which people have gotten into leadership positions, but have no real authority. Up to this point we have been talking about ways in which the flock gets abused, but there are ways in which the leadership gets abused, too. Understand, however, that this abuse still comes from the place of real authority and power, which is from those who decided the election. This view of the body of Christ can be illustrated with the following diagram:

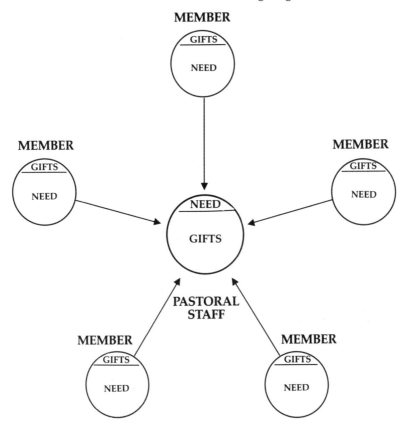

This is the church where people in the body have relationships with one another (the lines) and a focus on the pastor or paid staff (lines with arrows) to meet the needs of the members. The people in the church have little gifts and big needs, and the pastor has big gifts and little needs. Everyone looks to the pastor to get his needs met. ("After all, that's what we're paying him for.")

Since, in reality, the person in the center is *not* powerful enough to meet everyone's needs (and it is not even his job) he burns out. This person becomes exhausted trying to be big enough in the gift department to meet the needs of these "under-gifted" people. In the end, the people have power over the leader, though the leader may never realize it.

In many of these churches, we have noticed another amazing thing. People who are in the ministry are trusted, until they get paid. As soon as they receive a paycheck they become suspect immediately. The combination of this suspicion with the fact that those who have the job have no authority makes them pawns of the real power-brokers, consigned to the treadmill of performing ministry to justify their existence.

A healthy system looks like this:

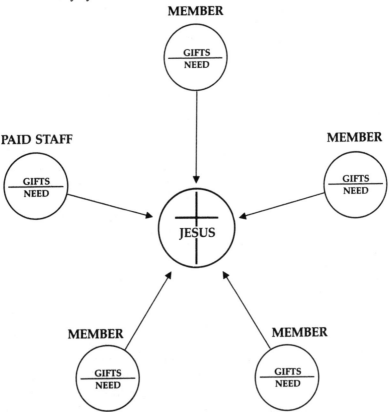

It is a body of many members, all with gifts and needs, interrelated and interdependent upon one another. The paid staff is on the outside of the circle just like everyone else. The reason some are paid is because they have training, experience, expertise. Not everyone else has this, nor do they need to. They need simply to contribute out of the gift God has given to them.

At the center of this system is Jesus. Can the True Head of the Church do anything He wants to at your church? Really? Anything? He is the Source and it is His Spirit we rely upon to meet needs. The people and the gifts are *resources* from the Source. When I come to the system with a need, the Holy Spirit energizes a gift through someone else to meet that need. God is the need-meeter, we are resources, no one burns out. In 1 Corinthians 12:11–12, 18, Paul says:

> But one and the same Spirit works all these things, distributing to each one individually just as He wills. For even as the body is one and yet has many members, and all the members of the body, though they are many, are one body, so also is Christ. But now God has placed the members, each one of them, in the body, just as He desired.

Responsibility and Authority

A spiritually abusive system is a place where people who have *responsibility* to do the job don't have the *authority* to do it. These people are being abused and will eventually burn out. In this kind of environment, there will be a group of people who posture power and exercise all of the authority to decide what needs to be done and how to do it. But they have very little responsibility to do anything. Combine this with a group of people who are responsible to do everything, but have no authority to decide how it gets done.

What happens, then, is that the person with all the responsibility and no authority is used up, burns out, and then is discarded.

In order for people to *not* burn out, and for the system to not be abusive, authority and responsibility to minister must both rest in the same place. This means that those who are given responsibility are also given authority.

For instance, one woman who is under me (Jeff speaking) organizationally has authority to do her ministry, even though I am her authority: It is her responsibility to facilitate our Women's Sexual Abuse support groups; therefore, she gets to decide how those are done. I don't decide how to do that. She's the expert on those things. I use my authority, power, resources and position to come under her and say, "What can I give you and how can I set you free to succeed in the ministry God wants you to do?" She has both the responsibility to perform the ministry and the authority to decide how it gets done.

Conclusion

We would like to leave you with three thoughts as we come to the close of this book.

First, you may have internal issues for which you need help and support, whether you leave or stay in your present spiritual system. Take care of yourself. It is all right to get help. "Blessed are the broken and mourning."

If, after all is said and done, you decide to leave the system because it is too abusive, your life will lighten up. But be careful that you don't think that changing geographical locations will solve all your issues. Find out how you got set up to be abused in the first place. And find relationships in which it is safe to heal from the wounds of the abuse.

Second, listen to God and do what He tells you. If you are a victim of spiritual abuse, this may be very hard. You have been taught to let everyone else speak for God, and you have been punished for trying to hear from God yourself. He may tell you to stay, when all of the evidence of abuse says to leave. He may even tell you to leave, when everything is going great. On the other hand, it may have been Him, not you, telling you to leave the abuse all along. And He will never leave you or forsake you. *Listen to God.*

We would like to close by referring you to the way the disciples responded to oppression. Acts 4:23 says, "And when they had been released, they went to their *own* companions, and reported all that the chief priests and elders had said to them."

When you experience spiritual abuse, find your own friends who understand and tell them about it. Get some support.

Consider their prayer in Acts 4:29–30:

And now, Lord, take note of their threats, and grant that Thy bond-servants may speak Thy word with all confidence, while Thou dost extend Thy hand to heal, and signs and wonders take place through the name of Thy holy Servant Jesus.

That is our prayer for you, too:

God, please pay attention to how those who have given their lives to serve you are getting intimidated and abused. And even in the middle of that, authorize and empower them to keep telling the truth. And keep moving your hand over your people to bring healing and rest, in the name of Jesus.

Epilogue

Message to Perpetrators of Spiritual Abuse

Just hours before Jesus violently purged the temple, Luke 19 tells us: "He saw the city [Jerusalem, and its temple], and wept over it." The reason? "You did not recognize your day of visitation" (v. 44). Jesus the Messiah was among His people. He spoke truth, offered life, hope and grace—and they did not want it. Instead of grace, they chose judgment.

Even so, it breaks the heart of God.

Jesus described Jerusalem as the one "who kills the prophets." The full weight of His anguish is felt when we realize the God-intended character of that city: Jerusalem was supposed to be known as the Holy City, the City of Peace, the Sanctuary of God, the hill of the Lord, the community of the righteous, beautiful for habitation. "Oh, Jerusalem, Jerusalem. You are not what you were created to be."

Do you think the grief of God is ever expressed that way toward the church? Do you wonder if He ever looks at spiritually abusive Christianity and says, "Oh, Beloved Eklesia, Redeemed of the Lord, Bride of Christ, Salt of the Earth. You are not what you were created to be. You are not the sanctuary of God or of man. You are not a safe place. You are not a holy place. You are not beautiful for habitation. You have tied heavy weights upon people, you have inverted values, and you have shut off the kingdom from those who were seeking it."

A Desire to "Gather"

We need constantly to be reminded that even when we have acted badly in the name of God, His heart is still to gather us to himself. When we relinquish our wrong control and turn to Him, He desires

233

most of all to redeem, heal and protect.

Even if you have abused others, God still extends His arms to you and says, "Come unto Me, all you who are weary and heavy-laden and I will give you rest."

Does this sound like a welcome invitation to you? We believe it is from the heart of God.

A Will of Our Own

Like arrogant, ignorant, rebellious children, however, we can sometimes resist to the end. We may think, "I don't need help, I don't need healing, I don't need grace. I'm doing quite well, thank you."

The problem with not responding to the "gathering" call of God is that it leaves you completely on your own. You are going to get what you wanted—no protection, no sustaining, no provision.

"Behold, your house is being left to you desolate," says Jeremiah 22:5. The word *desolate* means barren, vacant, uninhabited. God no longer plows, or plants, or prunes here.

Can that same dynamic happen today in the church? Is it possible that the Spirit of God could move among the churches and say to some of them, "This is not God's house, this is not God's work—it is *yours*"?

We are not "doom-sayers." Jesus loves His church! Therefore, He does not withdraw His hand quickly. He will send people who see the need to speak the truth, to lift the load, to heal the sheep. By His Spirit and through His Word, He will call and convict and draw to himself. For some, the result will be brokenness, mourning, and repentance— bringing life and restoration.

Though the desolation we may have wrought is real, we need only call upon Him again, welcoming back the grace we once received.

The "good news" is that God loves to give grace to people who know they need it!